A Job-Seeker's Guide
to Careers in
Market Research

March 2015 -
To David,
Best Regards,

A Job-Seeker's Guide to Careers in Market Research

James T. Heisler, PhD

Paramount Market Publishing, Inc.

Paramount Market Publishing, Inc.
950 Danby Road, Suite 136
Ithaca, NY 14850
www.paramountbooks.com
Voice: 607-275-8100; 888-787-8100 Fax: 607-275-8101

Publisher: James Madden
Editorial Director: Doris Walsh

ISBN 13: 978-1-941688-31-1 | ISBN 10: 1-941688-31-4

For

Rhonda

Contents

Introduction

"If you don't wake up in the morning excited to pick up where you left your work yesterday, you haven't found your calling yet."
—Mike Wallace, *CBS News*

Hundreds of thousands of people work in market research around the world. Some 400,000 of these market research jobs are in the U.S. It is safe to assume that as a child not one of these individuals ever uttered the words: "I want to be a market researcher when I grow up." Moreover, very few had ever heard of the industry, or wondered about a profession with it, until they were in college or beyond.

If you're like most people, you've come to market research through a serendipitous path. Perhaps you heard about it in a college course, became aware of public opinion polls, read some statistics in a news article, or were exposed to it while working in a related job. If you were particularly industrious, you may have done part-time interviewing to earn cash while in college.

The list of pathways is long and varied. A 2013 LinkedIn discussion among a number of market researchers focused on how they got into the field. The following are a sample of comments.

> "I found that at university I liked the research methods element of my degree best and also had a psychometric test indicating MR as my best career. Put them both together and there we go. I chose to go into the field. And happy that I did."

> "I used to be a chemist, I was doing research on new ingredients, and one day someone decided to hire me for market research. That's how I started, and never stopped! I like human beings better than molecules!"

> "I helped out at a MR company while studying—really enjoyed the environment and joined the company full time after completing my studies. 27 years later still doing market research."

> "I had a roommate in college who watched TV incessantly. While this may not seem remarkable, it was mostly the commercials he was watching. When I asked him why, he introduced me to something that sounded oxymoronic called 'marketing research.'"

> "I originally wanted to be a product manager after I obtained my MBA, but I graduated during one of the worst economic recessions of our time and I had to compete with what seemed like a gazillion other new graduates for an entry-level intern position at a small market research company in L.A. There I learned the art and science of MR. My plan was to stay in MR until the economy improved, thinking more PM positions would open up. I eventually landed a PM position in consumer products but found MR much more interesting and a better fit for me. Fortunately, I was able to find an MR slot on the client side. I have been a market researcher ever since. It was the right path for me."

In my own case, as a psychology major at the University of Michigan I had wondered what I could do with an advanced degree in the subject other than teach or "heal people." I first learned about market research in an undergraduate course in Consumer Behavior offered by the Economics department. I was a junior at the time. My professor was the renowned George Katona, a pioneer of economic psychology who devised a way to measure consumer expectations that eventually became the basis for the University of Michigan's highly regarded *Consumer Sentiment Index*. This index established its value and prominence when Katona employed it to accurately predict the post-WWII economic boom in the United States. At the time all conventional econometric indicators were predicting a recession.

The engaging Professor Katona opened my eyes to the field of market research and its connection to psychology. I was eager to know more. Lucky for me, I hailed from Chicago, a major metropolis with a well-established industry in advertising, marketing, and research. Over the next two summers I sought and found employment as a research intern at two small research companies, giving me roughly six months of exposure to the industry.

Working in boutique agencies turned out to be a stroke of luck in that I got a good overview of each organization and was exposed to a wide variety of tasks. I did everything from printing copies of questionnaires and reports (this was in the late 1960s, long before desktop publishing) to creating summary tables of survey findings, to eventually being trusted to write report chapters for client projects.

My first internship was with Creative Research Associates, where one of my most eye-opening and educational experiences came as a result of being given the decidedly unglamorous task of organizing the company's file room. I spent a good portion of that summer in a small room lined with shelves of file boxes containing old proposals, questionnaires, data tabs, and reports. At lunchtime, I would sit at a small table at one end of the room in front of a large window and examine the contents of some of these boxes. I simply read everything I could get my hands on. I was curious to find out what market researchers did and, more important, how they did it. Call it *learning through osmosis.* Since the staff at CRA was quite small, I had an opportunity to chat daily with the principal Saul Ben-Zeev, a pioneer of the focus group technique. He and his colleagues were great teachers and patiently answered all of my questions. It was a first-class learning experience.

The next year I found a second summer internship at a boutique firm called Behavioral Research, whose staff of sociologists were graduates of the University of Chicago. Once again, I was surrounded by and mentored by wonderful teachers. The company had a large contract to evaluate viewers' attitudes and perceptions of the ABC-TV stations in key geographic markets. I was tasked with analyzing and writing a section in the reports that focused on community reporting. I liked the responsibility and found the work engaging. By the end of that second summer I had found my career path.

That was over four decades ago. During the course of my career I have worked in junior and then senior roles for some of the biggest and most respected market research firms in the industry, as well as for lesser-known boutique firms and even start-ups. I have worked locally, regionally, nationally, and globally for private sector commercial clients and public sector (government) clients, for-profit businesses and not-for-profits. My work has focused on every marketing issue faced by these organizations.

Over the years I have asked many of these people how they ended up in market research. Most admit they just "stumbled into it." Regrettably, once in the field, the career path is not well lighted. There is very little time or effort given to educating entry-level practitioners about the various job functions, their skill requirements, how to progress through the industry, potential earning power, and many other essential facts. It seems that the market research industry counsels everyone on how to run their businesses but has ignored its own. I've tried to do my part on occasion, speaking to psychology and business school graduate students about market research as a career. This book draws on my own experience, as well as that of my colleagues and clients, to provide a roadmap for aspiring researchers.

This book is a practical career guide: how to enter the field and how to carve out a successful career that makes the most of your own special skills, aptitudes, and interests. It is not a comprehensive textbook that explains in detail how to do market research. That's a topic for much longer books or an academic curriculum devoted to the subject, like the six-course graduate certificate program I have developed for the Petrocelli College of Continuing Studies at Fairleigh Dickinson University in New Jersey.

My purpose here is to paint an accurate picture of the market research industry at the beginning of the 21st century—its size and scope, what value it provides, who works in the field, who uses it and for what decisions, the market research process, common methodologies, growth prospects for the industry, and what lies ahead. Having set the context, we will then shift focus to market research as a career choice—requisite skills, education, and training; where the jobs are, how to get that first job, what you are likely to do as an entry-level employee, moving onward and upward, potential earning power, success profiles, and stepping stones to related careers.

At the end of our journey together, you should have a good understanding of the industry and be able to make an informed assessment of whether this is a career you want to pursue.

My former colleague and industry heavyweight, Richard M. Johnson, in looking back on his own career in market research had this to say about his trajectory:

"I have had an interesting and rewarding career in marketing research that has been somewhere on the boundary between the academic and the practical. A lesson from my experience is that young people should keep their minds open about career choices and avoid foreclosing any possible paths of development. They may not learn until later in life what their most satisfying calling is."

—*Journal of Marketing Research*, October 15, 2005

One final note is warranted. While the market research industry's roots have been largely in the United States, pioneering work also has been done elsewhere in the world. Today the industry is truly global in terms of those who conduct market research, those who take the surveys, and those who use the information. Nevertheless, much of what I have to say is focused in the United States.

JAMES T. HEISLER, PhD
SKILLMAN, NEW JERSEY

PART 1

The Market Research Industry

"Advertising people who ignore research are as dangerous as generals who ignore decodes of enemy signals."

—David Ogilvy

legendary 20th-century advertising executive

CHAPTER 1

What is Market Research?

Let's begin with a dense but useful definition offered by the American Marketing Association:

> "Marketing research is the function that links the consumer, customer, and public to the marketer through information—information used to identify and define marketing opportunities and problems; generate, refine, and evaluate marketing actions; monitor marketing performance; and improve understanding of marketing as a process. Marketing research specifies the information required to address these issues, designs the method for collecting information, manages and implements the data collection process, analyzes the results, and communicates the findings and their implications."

Looking for a streamlined definition that gets to the real value of the discipline? Let me offer this one: market research helps organizations make well-informed decisions.

Let's take these definitions one step further. While the discipline of market research, as stated above, includes the world of public opinion polling and social research, this book focuses on careers that support the marketing process, whether for public or private sector organizations (both for-profit and non-profit).

I have often described market research as serving a "middle man" function between any organization and its constituents, the purpose being to enable a win-win scenario for both parties.

Numerous critics chastised the advertising and marketing industries in the late 1950s and early 1960s for allegedly manipulating people's desires for products and services. In the U.S. one of the most vocal critics was the journalist and author Vance Packard (1914-1996). In his vastly popular books like *The Hidden Persuaders* (1957) and *The Waste Makers* (1960) he claimed that advertisers used consumer motivational research (i.e., market research) and psychological techniques to manipulate consumers' expectations to induce a desire for specific products. He identified eight "compelling needs" that advertisers promise products will fulfill. According to Packard, these needs—**Emotional Security, Reassurance of Worth, Ego Gratification, Creativity, Love Objects, Sense of Power, Roots,** and **Immortality**—are so strong that people are compelled to buy goods and services to satisfy them, products they didn't even know they needed.

> MARKET RESEARCH helps organizations make well-informed decisions.

My goal is not to challenge the veracity of Packard's argument about what the *Mad Men* of the 1950s and 1960s were up to. However, the discipline of market research as used by today's advertisers and marketers is broader and more well-intentioned. It helps inform and assess an organization's business strategies and tactics. It provides information about the relevant needs, wants, attitudes, perceptions, and behaviors of constituents so the organization can create, communicate, and deliver products, services, and experiences that meet its customers' wants and expectations. It makes for a better, more satisfying transaction, a win-win for both the customer and the company.

For skeptics who may say "we know all that already," market research helps companies see opportunities and avoid mistakes. This is accomplished by analyzing existing data (e.g., census data, scanner data, financial trends, sales data, existing databases, social media, etc.) and through standard survey research practices. Such surveys collect data from a defined group of people who are sampled from a larger pool of this target group. The selected individuals are asked a set of carefully-designed questions. The results are then tabulated and analyzed by one or more statistical procedures and then reported. More about all of this later.

> MARKET RESEARCH provides information about relevant needs, wants, attitudes, perceptions, and behaviors of constituents so the organization can create, communicate, and deliver products, services, and experiences that meet its customers' wants and expectations.

Today the world of market research is a $39 billion per year global industry. Closely linked to the ups and downs of the world economy, the industry is reported to be growing, according to ESOMAR (the European Society for Opinion and Market Research) in its 2013 annual report on the state of the global market research industry. Year-over-year revenue grew by 3.2 percent (0.7 percent after adjustment for inflation). By far the largest growth is taking place in rapidly expanding economies in Latin America, Asia Pacific, and Africa. At the same time, the two primary geographic markets for market research—Europe and North America—saw a slight drop and no change, respectively.

Global Market Research Turnover 2012
$39 Billion Revenue

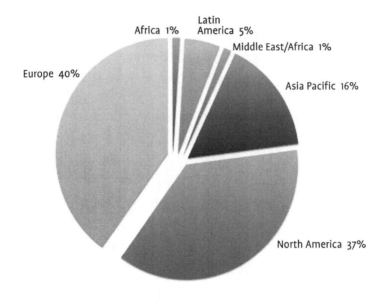

Source: ESOMAR 2013

Every year many millions of people are surveyed about a vast spectrum of issues, attitudes, perceptions, behaviors, wants, and opinions. The impact of market research is felt in every facet of our daily lives, from the nature of the products and services we buy and use; to the messages, prices, and channels through which they are delivered to us; to helping to define and shape public opinion; to whom we elect as our leaders.

The Who, What, How, and How

I like to sum it up this way: market research essentially answers four key questions that together provide a comprehensive snapshot of the entire marketing process. Let's call these the **Who, What, How,** and **How.** Here's a brief synopsis, but we will take up each of these questions in more detail later in the book.

QUESTION 1

Who Is the Audience for Our Product, Service or Message?

Here the organization sponsoring the research wants to know who (i.e., which individuals, groups, or organizations) will be most receptive to what they are seeking to do. The sponsor's goal may be to market a product or service or communicate a point of view about an issue. A typical survey focusing on this question may collect a large amount of information from a sample of people or organizations about their needs, wants, attitudes, behaviors, and usage of the product or service category in question. The subsequent analysis of the data may involve segmenting the surveyed respondents into groups differentiated on the basis of their characteristics, behaviors, or how they think. The findings help the sponsor identify who is the optimal audience for the product or service or message or tailor the offer or message to each subgroup.

QUESTION 2

What Should the Product or Service Look Like?

Here the goal is to design the offer to appeal to its intended audience. A sample of targeted consumers or businesses may be asked to react to different descriptions of the offer's features and functions in order to identify the optimal configuration that best meets the target's needs and expectations. Such research often employs sophisticated decision modeling techniques (e.g., discrete choice, MaxDiff, etc.) that force survey respondents to decide what they really value in a product or service. No offering can meet all needs and expectations; it's just not realistic.

QUESTION 3

How Do We Take Our Product or Service to Market?

Okay, we know our audience and have designed what we believe will be a winning product or service. The next question is how do we price it, position it vis-à-vis the competition, and talk about it? This is where advertising and brand research come into play. Here the audience identified in Question 1 may be shown ideas for advertisements and asked to react to them. Or they may be asked questions about their perceptions of one or more brands or what is often called brand imagery. Still other research involves sophisticated methodologies (e.g., conjoint analysis, van Westendorp price sensitivity, etc.) to define the optimal price points that will resonate with customers.

QUESTION 4

How Well Are We Doing?

Having gone to market with what the organization hopes is a winning proposition, the business needs to periodically find out how well it is performing. Is it meeting constituents' needs and expectations? What kinds of experiences is the business delivering to its customers? This is the realm of customer relationship research. This research may take the form of short customer surveys after using the product or service in question or interacting with the brand, e.g., call to customer support. All of us are familiar—likely too familiar—with incessant requests for customer feedback each time we make an online purchase, buy a restaurant meal, fly on a plane, stay in a hotel, or make a purchase at one of the big brick-and-mortar retailers. Customers also are often asked to participate in longer surveys that focus more on the overall experiences that the business is delivering.

In the 1880s, John Wanamaker, the famed East Coast department store magnate, said "Half the money I spend on advertising is wasted; the trouble is I don't know which half." Market research would have helped Mr. Wanamaker answer that question.

Science or Art?

Finally, I earlier described market research as performing a "middle man" function. There is one other description I have often used. I like to say that market research is one part science and two parts art. The science of market research is inherent in its use of statistics and well-recognized psychological constructs about attitudes, perceptions, and group behaviors, as well as psychology's methodologies for posing questions and using scales. All of this provides structure to the traditional market research process.

> The purpose of market research is to help an organization succeed by providing it with empirical market-based information to MINIMIZE THE RISKS associated with all the decisions it must make to take its products and services to market.

The goal of market research is to understand and predict human behavior. Although the science available to us is getting better at enabling market researchers to achieve this goal, we still have a long way to go. Researchers are sometimes left to sift through reams of conflicting or ambiguous data and make a "best effort" interpretation. This is particularly true when data are generated by relatively new sources such as social media and Big Data. These sources are, by nature, very unstructured. So this is where the "art" comes in, and this, in part, is what makes market research so exciting.

CHAPTER 2

Market Research:
A Brief Look Back

The history of the market research industry is told more by way of anecdotes than hard facts. Nevertheless, there are some known facts and milestones. Let's take a look at a few of these.

While the formal practice of market research is relatively young, it's safe to say that its roots date back centuries. It has been said that even the Israelites sent interviewers into the markets of Canaan to sample the goods (Lawrence C. Lockley, *Journal of Marketing*, Vol. 14. No. 5, April 1950, p733).

Herodotus, who lived in 5th century BC Greece and is sometimes referred to as the first historian, is said to have travelled the world and occasionally interviewed the people he encountered. In his book titled *The Histories*, Herodotus provides a discourse on the world from its mythical origins, to empires won and lost, to its geography. His narrative is both first-person, based on his own experiences, as well as second-hand, based on accounts from those he has met in his extensive travels.

We have to fast-forward in time to see evidence of efforts to conduct "scientific" surveys. Most evidence is associated with politics. We know, for example, that during Thomas Jefferson's presidency (1801-1809), there was regular canvassing of voters to determine their voting intentions. There is no evidence, however, that questions were asked about the voters' attitudes or demographics. In 1824 the first recorded straw vote appeared in a newspaper, *The Harrisburg Pennsylvanian* announcing that Andrew Jackson was the favored presidential candidate. Chicago newspapers in 1896 conducted straw polls to determine the outcome of the McKinley-Bryan presidential election.

Industry Pioneers

Market research as a formalized industry began in the U.S. in the 1920s, the heyday of radio advertising. It was at this time that consumer product manufacturers began to realize the importance of understanding demographics. Various companies sought to sponsor different radio programs in order to present their advertising message to different segments of the listening public.

Some call **Charles Coolidge Parlin** (1872–1942) the father of market research. In any case he is among its first professional practitioners. Parlin was employed by the Curtis Publishing Company to gather ongoing information about customers and markets in order to help the company sell more advertising in its popular weekly magazine, *The Saturday Evening Post*. He went on to found the pioneering commercial market research company, National Analysts, which was spun off by Curtis Publishing in 1943 to provide market research services to businesses and government. National Analysts was renamed Naxion in 2014. The Charles Coolidge Parlin Marketing Research Award was established in 1945 by "the Philadelphia Chapter of the AMA (American Marketing Association) and The Wharton

School in association with the Curtis Publishing Company to honor persons who have made outstanding contributions to the field of marketing research."

Others say that the title "father of market research" belongs to **Daniel Starch** (1883–1979), an American psychologist and marketer. While Parlin's focus was on the demographic profiles of those who read various publications, Starch focused on what people remembered from the ads that appeared in those publications. In the 1930s Starch developed a research methodology that collected information on advertising recognition. This information was indexed against the known circulation of the publication as a way to let advertisers see how effective their ads were in reaching their target audiences.

Another industry pioneer and icon, **George Gallup** (1901–1984), developed a variation on Starch's methodology which, unlike Starch's approach, did not require interviewers to actually show respondents the advertisements in question. Gallup is best known for his pioneering work in public opinion polling. In 1935 he founded the Gallup Organization in Princeton, New Jersey. His goal was to measure public opinion objectively. He underscored his independence by refusing to do any polling that was paid for or sponsored by any special interest groups such as political parties. (Times have certainly changed! Today political polling is a huge industry.) In 1936 Gallup successfully predicted that Franklin Roosevelt would defeat Alfred Landon for the U.S. presidency. By 1938 Gallup and his vice president, **David Ogilvy** (who later went on to become a giant in the advertising industry), began conducting market research for advertising companies.

The venerable George Gallup had another colleague by the name of **Claude Robinson**. The story goes that Claude Robinson split off from Gallup in 1938 to found Opinion Research Corporation (ORC) for the purpose of applying marketing research to business issues, not just advertising effectiveness. One area of interest was researching the customers of businesses that sold goods and services to other businesses. Today we call this the business-to-business (B2B) space. Some time later Robinson partnered with Gallup again. In 1948 the two founded Gallup and Robinson, a firm specializing in advertising research. Robinson never walked away from his roots in public opinion polling. In 1960 he was Richard Nixon's pollster in his unsuccessful presidential bid against John F. Kennedy. Robinson died at an early age in 1961.

I had the pleasure of spending almost half of my career at ORC. I was hired in 1982 to run the company's Washington, D.C. office, moved in 1993 to the Princeton, New Jersey, headquarters office, and rose to the rank of Executive Vice President before leaving the company in 2001 to take a position with a small boutique company called Hase Schannen. ORC continues today as one of the largest and most recognized firms in the industry. Over its long history it has spawned other research companies (among them, Total Research, Response Analysis, Research 100) as principals peeled away to start their own firms. Many of these entrepreneurs stayed in the area because of longstanding community ties and because there was an excellent pool of experienced, talented professionals to draw from in and around the town. As a result, Princeton—a town of less than 30,000 individuals but part of a much larger metropolitan area stretching from Philadelphia to New York City—became known not only for its world-class university, but also as a major hub of the U.S. market research industry.

In the 1950s market research began to get more sophisticated. Studies went beyond observing and reporting consumer behavior and began to delve into how consumers think—their motives, influences, process of decision-making, etc. In so doing, market research became increasingly integral to all aspects of marketing, helping guide decisions on what products and services to take to market, whom to market them to, product positioning, pricing, and distribution. Continuing on into the 1960s and 1970s, the field was marked not so much by how data were collected or for what purpose, but by advances in statistical procedures to draw deep insights from the data. Later in this book we'll look at some of the work done with respect to **decision modeling.**

Following World War II and into the 1970s, the industry grew with the emergence of new firms, many spun-off of other firms. Some of these companies billed themselves as full-service, doing any kind of research that a client needed. Others became niche players focusing on specific issues such as advertising research, package testing, B2B, qualitative, and so on.

Technology Drives Methodology

Like many fields, market research has gone through tremendous technological changes over time. The practice of conducting surveys by mail was noted as far back as the mid-1800s (Christopher Scott, *Journal of the Royal Statistical Society*, Series A [General] 1961). Printed questionnaires were mailed to people's homes or places of businesses.

An Interviewer from the ancient world

Once completed, the respondent then mailed the survey back to its sponsor. This method of data collection continues today, used widely by public sector organizations but rarely by businesses. At the same time, people were interviewed in person in their homes or in public spaces by interviewers using clipboards and paper questionnaires.

In the 1970s and 1980s telephone surveys began to replace both mailed and in-person surveys. This phenomenon was facilitated by the creation of a telephone technology called **Wide Area Telephone Service (WATS)**. This service enabled long-distance calling at a flat rate, thus making data collection by telephone interviewing more affordable. Phone surveys became the dominant mode of data collection up to the mid-1990s.

In 1995 desktop computing and the Internet began to revolutionize market research, and over the past two decades the pace of change has quickened in ways the early industry pioneers could never have imagined. The industry is evolving quickly both technologically and methodologically, from the means of collecting data, to the type of data collected, to how we analyze it and report the findings. Most respondents today are recruited online through email invitations and complete surveys online, sometimes on a mobile device. Some respondents participate in online panels of consumers, professionals, or business executives.

We are living in an era of passive collection of data via GPS. Based on your location, stores can send a coupon or survey to your mobile phone. This enables researchers to gather real-time feedback on a product or service experience. They can even interact with the consumer as they shop, asking them to look at a label or take photos of what they are buying.

Answers to surveys no longer need to be verbal. In addition to asking respondents to provide photographs, we can use things like the Facebook widgets (like 👍 and dislike 👎), first seen in 2007.

Social media provides a vast new body of data for researchers to analyze. A software methodology known as **text analysis** allows us to "mine" social media commentary to identify themes and the sentiment behind these themes. More about this methodology in Chapter 7.

The four basic questions remain the same—**WHO, WHAT, HOW, and HOW.** But as technology enables companies and public institutions to gather data about our personal transactions, experiences, preferences, and habits without our tacit permission, we have entered a new and different—and some would say alarming—territory, a world where our privacy is for sale, or at any rate is traded away for convenience and possibly national security.

This issue of privacy will be an ever larger topic within the field of market research as the industry turns its focus increasingly towards non-survey types of data (e.g., social media, **Big Data**). Survey respondents' privacy has long been protected through guidelines set by CASRO (Council of American Survey Research Organizations) and others. For example, respondents are guaranteed anonymity unless they give their permission to share their responses with the survey sponsor. Non-survey data is an entirely different realm. Some would say it is a far more sensitive realm in that we are talking about personal behaviors. Undoubtedly, as time goes on there will be cries for increased protections surrounding data mining which will lead to restrictions on what kinds of data can be captured and reported.

> As TECHNOLOGY enables companies and public institutions to gather data about our personal transactions, experiences, preferences, and habits without our tacit permission, we have entered a new and different – and some would say alarming – territory.

Market Research Goes Global

While much of the market research industry traces its roots to the U.S., there was academic research taking place in Austria and Germany in the early part of the 20th century. **Paul Lazarsfeld**, who worked at the Office of Economic-Psychological Research at the University of Vienna (1927–1934), was one of the early pioneers in consumer research in Europe. He later migrated to the U.S. It wasn't until after the Second World War that market research took root throughout Europe and spread to other parts of the world.

Today market research is done in virtually every country, and every major market research supplier has affiliate offices around the globe. Nielsen, the largest company, has offices in 105 countries. In addition, there are hundreds, if not thousands, of home-grown research agencies throughout the world.

All companies research essentially the same issues and use the same methodologies. However, there are some technological, social, and cultural differences across geographic regions that impact the practice of market research. For example, Internet usage, while growing, is not as pervasive in many developing countries as it is elsewhere. This can restrict the use of online surveys in those countries. In the 1990s it was not culturally acceptable to conduct telephone interviews with business people. The interviews had to be done in-person by appointment. ESOMAR's *Guideline for Online Research, 2011* provides details on privacy regulations for online surveys throughout Europe.

Finally, there are differences in how survey respondents use rating scales in surveys. For example, Asians and those in Latin America tend to be high raters, whereas Northern Europeans are typically low markers. Therefore, one has to be careful when comparing survey results across countries. For example, the fact that customer satisfaction scores are much higher in Japan than in England may reflect nothing more than the differences in how the Japanese and the British use rating scales.

CHAPTER 3

The Consumers of Market Research

Reliance on market research is pervasive worldwide. The consumers of market research are organizations large and small, for-profit and non-profit, providers of products or services, proponents of a particular issue or cause, as well as federal, state, and local government agencies. Within the private sector, market research is commissioned by every industry sector serving both consumers and business-to-business. The very biggest users tend to be providers of consumer packaged and hard goods, as well as the pharmaceutical industry. These companies spend millions of dollars commissioning original, proprietary studies, referred to as **primary or custom research,** as well as purchase existing reports, referred to as **secondary or syndicated research.**

In business, the end users of market research are typically people working in product or service design and marketing and sales functions. Many firms today have at least one or two employees whose job it is to commission research and then translate the findings back to senior management. A big consumer goods (e.g., General Foods) and services (e.g., Bank of America) company may employ scores of people in its market research function, now often referred to as the Market Insights group.

In 2012 expenditures for all types of market research by industry sector looked like this:

Sources of Market Research Spending 2012

Sales by Industry Sector

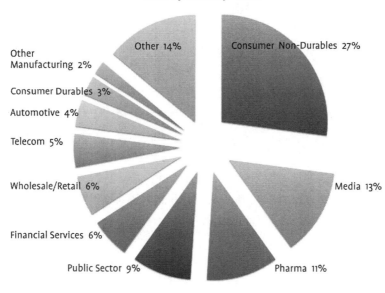

Other 14%

Consumer Non-Durables 27%

Other Manufacturing 2%

Consumer Durables 3%

Automotive 4%

Telecom 5%

Wholesale/Retail 6%

Media 13%

Financial Services 6%

Public Sector 9%

Pharma 11%

Source: ESOMAR 2013

It is the rare organization that doesn't commission some sort of formal market research Intelligence at least once a year. So ingrained is market research in the DNA of how organizations operate today that there has been considerable research conducted about market research. In a series of studies and papers published in 1992,* Gerald Zaltman of the Harvard Business School, along with associates, examined various aspects of the relationship between providers and

---

* "Relationships between Providers and Users of Market Research: The Dynamics of Trust Within and Between Organizations" (*Journal of Marketing Research [JMR]* 29, no.3, August 1992: 314-328).

users of market research. In one such study, the authors described a comprehensive theory of trust in market research relationships. This theory focused on the factors that determine users' trust in their researchers, including individual, interpersonal, organizational, and project factors. The theory was tested in a sample of 779 users of market research. Results indicated that interpersonal factors are the most predictive of trust. Among these factors, perceived researcher integrity, willingness to reduce research uncertainty, expertise, tactfulness, sincerity, congeniality, and timeliness were most strongly associated with confidentiality and trust. Zaltman and his colleagues found that trust had a positive impact on the degree to which the research was used by those who had commissioned it. Needless to say, this is worth noting by aspiring market researchers.

> Perceived researcher integrity, willingness to reduce research uncertainty, expertise, tactfulness, sincerity, congeniality, and timeliness were most strongly associated with CONFIDENTIALITY AND TRUST.

It also is important to understand what the buyers of market research want to buy. Theodore Levitt, the famous economist and Harvard Business School professor, was well-known for, among other things, his pithy remarks. One of Levitt's oft-quoted gems, probably one of the most famous in all of marketing, was "people don't want a quarter-inch drill; they want a quarter-inch hole." The consumers of market research don't want a research project, they want knowledge and insight. What Levitt was saying is that marketing must focus on the buyers' wants and needs, not on the product per se.

Not surprisingly, there has been increasing emphasis on market research results that are **actionable, provide a return on investment (ROI),** and **reduce risk.** Research projects that fail to meet one or more of these criteria are often left on a shelf to collect dust.

Actionable Research

It is the rare buyer and seller of market research who doesn't use the term "actionable results" at least once in a request for a proposal and in the responding proposal. What exactly is meant by "actionable?" In short, users of market research want a report of the findings that clearly tells them what they need to do in response to the business question(s) being addressed and, in some cases, what is likely to happen in the marketplace as a result.

The following is an example from customer relationship research. At the core of every customer relationship survey is 1) a measure of loyalty and 2) the identification of the relative impact that various aspects of the customer experience (e.g., sales, support, communications, billing, etc.) have on driving that measure. Using standard **regression techniques**, researchers can show the client what might happen in

> CONSUMERS of market research don't want a research project, they want knowledge and insight.

terms of increased customer loyalty if the business were to increase customers' perceptions of its performance by X, Y, or Z percentage points on each of these customer experience elements. In other words, an analysis of the data can tell the client which parts of the customer experience can be manipulated to increase customer loyalty and what might happen if they were to push those levers.

The ROI of Market Research

One of the best examples of the ROI of research was a 2004 study my team and I did for Pitney Bowes, the manufacturer of office mailing equipment and services. The company asked us to examine each of the ways it interacted with its business customers (e.g., sales, account management, support, billing, website, etc.). These incidences of business-customer interface are called **touchpoints**. The purpose of the research was to help Pitney Bowes retool its customers' experiences, each touchpoint, in light of what these customers wanted. What we found, and what is often found in such research, is that Pitney Bowes was over-delivering on some customer experiences. In other words, they were doing more than what customers wanted or expected in order to keep them satisfied. In terms of one touchpoint, account management, Pitney Bowes was having its account reps personally visit their customers' offices four times a year. The research showed that these 200,000 customers didn't need an account rep to make an in-person visit and preferred that the business follow-up be handled by a phone call. As a result, the company migrated this key account management function to a call center. In so doing, they cut the costs exponentially. Let's just say that the savings paid for the research investment many times over. This is a classic example of the value of market research.

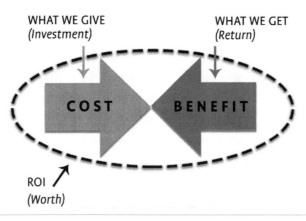

WHAT WE GIVE
(Investment)

WHAT WE GET
(Return)

COST

BENEFIT

ROI
(Worth)

Source: © 2012 Research Management Systems

Reducing Risk

Market research doesn't guarantee success. However, going to market with products, services, and messages BEFORE taking into account the insights gained by conducting well-constructed research substantially increases the risk of failure. It is the fundamental premise of marketing—provide customers with what they want and need. The role of market research is to facilitate this goal.

What Kinds of Research Are Clients Buying?

Market research buyers are spending the largest share of their budgets on proprietary quantitative research. Within this bucket, the WHO question—Who is the audience for our product, service, or message? (i.e., Usage and Attitudes, Market Measurement)—gets the largest share of spend. The first HOW question—How do we take our product or service to market? (i.e., Advertising Pre-Testing, Advertising/Brand Tracking, Media Audience) and the WHAT question—What should the product or service look like? (i.e., Market Modeling, New Product/ Service)—follow. The second HOW question—How well are we doing? (i.e., Stakeholder Measurement)—gets the smallest proportion of the overall research spend.

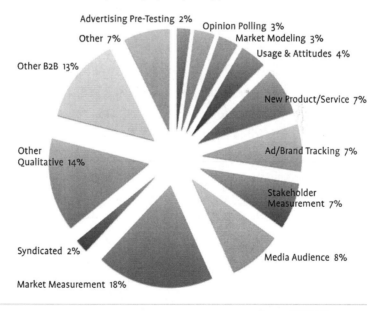

Spending by Project Type 2012

Advertising Pre-Testing 2%
Opinion Polling 3%
Other 7%
Market Modeling 3%
Usage & Attitudes 4%
Other B2B 13%
New Product/Service 7%
Other Qualitative 14%
Ad/Brand Tracking 7%
Stakeholder Measurement 7%
Syndicated 2%
Media Audience 8%
Market Measurement 18%

Source: ESOMAR 2013

CHAPTER 4

Market Research: The Big Picture

In this chapter we'll look at the different types of market research that are conducted and learn what goes into designing, executing, and reporting a market research project. The intent is not to provide a how-to manual on methodology—that's the job of a market research textbook or a sequence of course work—but to acquaint you with the broad goals of market research as a way of explaining what researchers do on the job. You'll see that the day-to-day tasks are varied and intellectually engaging. Some of the jobs are internal and some require constant client contact. All require teamwork of the highest order. Perhaps you'll see how your interests, aptitudes, and skills make you well suited for one or more of the roles described.

There are many categories of market research, as shown in the chart below, but they all come down to two basic categories: syndicated research and custom research. We begin with a distinction between these two basic categories.

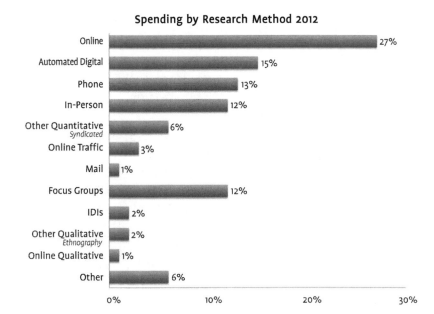

Spending by Research Method 2012

Source: ESOMAR 2013

Syndicated Versus Custom Research

In **syndicated research** information is collected through surveys or behavioral measures (e.g., monitoring of websites visited, scanning of sales receipts, self-reported diaries, etc.), analyzed, reported, and sold many times over to anyone willing to pay for the information. The focus of such research covers the full gamut of issues addressed by market research. Well-known examples are customer satisfaction data sold by J.D. Power; TV viewership data, brand awareness data, and supermarket scanner data sold by Nielsen; prescription data sold by IMS; and countless industry trend reports sold by companies like Gartner and Frost & Sullivan.

The key benefit to clients is that syndicated research provides a cost-effective way to obtain critical market intelligence. The trade-off is that the buyer has little, if any, input on the questions asked. Other typical benefits are as follows:

• Market Overview	Provides a representative view of the total market
• Industry Trends	Provides a macro-level perspective on issues enabling the buyer to understand the total market landscape
• Brand Awareness, Perceptions, and Competitive Positioning	Enables buyers to see how their brands are performing vis-à-vis the competition
• Competitive Intelligence	Provides the buyer with macro-level trends and details on specific issues

In **custom research** the project is sponsored by an organization for its own proprietary use to address one or more very specific business questions. The buyer of this research has total control of the scope, content, methodology, and deliverables. Custom research is further sub-divided into two categories: qualitative and quantitative.

Qualitative Research

Qualitative research collects information from a relatively small group of selected individuals who are asked to respond to a set of in-depth questions in their own words. The goal of this type of research is to uncover *what* people think about a particular product, service, issue rather than *how many* think this way. The most common means of collecting this type of information is either the **focus group** or the **in-depth interview** (**IDI,** conducted with one individual at a time).

Qualitative research may be all that is ever done to study a marketing issue. However, it is frequently used in conjunction with quantitative research. Typically qualitative research is done as a first step as a means of identifying **testable hypotheses** and guidelines for the development of the survey questionnaire. Bob Pankauskas, Director of Consumer Insights at Allstate Insurance, had this to say about the use of qualitative research in conjunction with quantitative research.

"You have to work a little harder to get insights out of a quantita-tive approach, so using qualitative helps a great deal. Our CMO will say, 'Great, what's the consumer insight? What is the pain point?' We need to focus on the problem we're solving for the customer. It's very easy to ask but often we find we're solving a problem for Allstate and not really solving the problem for con-sumers. We work hard to address that."*

The Focus Group

A focus group typically involves 8 to 12 people who have been screened to meet some particular criteria (e.g., purchasers of a certain product, specific demographics, etc.). The discussion is led by a trained mod-erator working from a script. Over a period of 90 to 120 minutes, the moderator's job is to pose questions in a non-leading fashion, probe responses (e.g., "Tell me more why you feel that way") to elicit a full understanding of the participants' comments, encourage everyone to participate, and steer the conversation across a range of questions that encompass the client's need to know.

The "data" collected take the form of hours of audio- and videotaped verbatim comments. The information is not subjected to statistical analysis. Rather, the individual(s) analyzing the discussions are looking for big themes (e.g., the new product concept appears to fill a need in the marketplace) and for patterns across participants (either consensus or differences), particularly types of participants (e.g., men appear to be more favorable to the idea than are women). Conclusions drawn from focus group research typically are stated as working hypotheses. This reflects the fact that the findings are based on the comments of a relatively small set of individuals. It is not known whether such attitudes, perceptions, behaviors are exhibited by many or few in the broader population. That investigation becomes the subject of a follow-up (more number-focused) quantitative research undertaking.

*Quirk's Marketing Review (August 2014).

Focus group methodology has been around for a long time and continues to be used extensively. What has changed over the years is more a matter of style and form, in an interesting comment on societal and technological changes. I observed my first focus group back in the 1970s and personally went on to moderate over 500 groups throughout the years. I observed scores more. Back in the "old days," men and women rarely participated in the same discussion. This wasn't so much a conceptual issue as a practical one. Most women, at least those of interest to marketers, were at home during the day. So focus groups with women were typically scheduled during the day, while those with men were done in the evening after work hours. Focus group participants are compensated for their time. Back then women were paid $5 and men $10! Presumably, the latter's time was considered to be more valuable.

It wasn't until the 1980s that specialized facilities for group discussions began to appear. Until then, it was not unusual to hold focus groups in people's homes or in general meeting spaces like those found in clubs, churches, or restaurants. Back then I moderated many groups with participants sitting around in a circle on bridge chairs with an old-fashioned reel-to-reel tape recorder positioned in the center of the circle to capture every word. I once moderated some groups on behalf of a major retailer who was interested in hearing the opinions of college students. I remember visiting a group of students in an apartment on campus. We sat around on whatever was available—chairs, couches, the floor. In order to build rapport with the respondents, a critical task for any moderator, I sat on the floor.

Fast forward to today where we have modern facilities built with the express purpose of facilitating the focus group experience. Clients sit behind one-way mirrors and every word and facial expression is captured on high-definition video. Today's groups are usually done only in the evening with men and women participating together, and both are paid the same. Economics also have caught up. That $5 and $10 incentive is now $50, $100, or more. However, one thing that hasn't changed is that you'll still find big bowls of candy set out for the clients observing from behind the one-way glass.

The vast majority of in-person focus groups run just as planned. The first few minutes are spent going around the table, each person introducing herself or himself. The moderator then introduces the topics and explains the ground rules—we want to hear everyone's thoughts about the topic, there are no right or wrong answers, feel free to comment on each other's thoughts, the discussion is being recorded and, yes, that is a mirror and my clients are sitting behind it. Let's all wave at them and now forget about them.

Ninety minutes later all the questions have been asked and the discussion, having started out broadly (e.g., "What kind of car does everyone drive?"), has zeroed in on the very specific topic in question (e.g., the client's new navigation system for cars). As expected, a few people have dominated the dialogue and at least one or two individuals had to be repeatedly encouraged to express their point of view. Mission accomplished.

Sometimes, things go awry. Any moderator who has been running focus groups for any length of time will have a collection of funny and not-so-funny anecdotes. In a group I conducted one evening the power failed 30 minutes into the discussion, leaving nine individuals sitting around a table in the dark. We waited several minutes, and then made the show-business-like decision to press on. We lit some candles and proceeded to conduct the discussion for another hour.

Sometimes participants do not behave themselves. I was running a focus group one evening when I couldn't help noticing that a man to my left had his arm behind the chair of the woman next to him, and she looked a bit uncomfortable with this show of familiarity. What really caught my attention, however, was the fact that his commentary was so bizarre that he was beginning to annoy all the other participants. I pushed on for a while and then made a decision that I had never made before or since: I decided to expel him from the group. I interrupted the discussion and said to the offender (we'll call him Joe), "I'm sorry, Joe, but I have to ask you to leave." I escorted him to the door and asked a colleague to pay him and show him out. I wasn't sure what I was going to find when I returned to the group. Fortunately, the rest of the participants expressed relief.

The Online Focus Group

It's increasingly common for focus groups to be conducted online. This approach addresses some of the drawbacks of traditional face-to-face discussions. Over two or three days some two dozen recruited participants take part in an ongoing discussion moderated by a professional who posts questions online. The participants provide their responses online and comment on what others are saying. Clients can follow the discussion 24/7 via their computers or devices and pose questions to the moderator throughout.

There are several key benefits of the online approach. People can be recruited from diverse geographies to participate in the same discussion. You avoid expensive travel costs for clients and moderator. It's unlikely that one or two people will dominate the discussion, as sometimes occurs in a face-to-face group. Each participant provides more commentary than in a traditional focus group discussion. The last point is particularly important. In a traditional focus group, the moderator will turn to others in the group and ask what they think. Participants might simply say "I agree." Online each participant is more likely to state a fully articulated opinion.

The In-Depth Interview

The one-on-one form of qualitative research, often referred to as an **in-depth interview (IDI),** is more often used in business-to-business research (B2B). That's because the participants are professionals or business executives who may be difficult to recruit into a group situation or may be reluctant to discuss organizational issues in front of others. As in the focus group format, the interviewer works from a topic guide, poses questions in a logical order, and records the respondent's comments. Such interviews typically run for 30 to 60 minutes and may be done over the telephone or in person.

Quantitative Research

The majority of market research investigations involve some type of **quantitative** approach (i.e., a survey). Here the goal is to quantify the issues in question, then describe and explain the data through statistical analyses. A targeted group of individuals numbering in the hundreds to thousands is asked to respond to a set of specific questions. The answers are tabulated and may be submitted to some form of statistical analysis. The findings are then summarized in a written report featuring numerical tables, graphs, and insightful commentary. Let's take a deeper look at the individual components of this type of research.

The questionnaire or "survey instrument" is the heart of a survey. It is the list of questions that answer the client's business question(s). There is a science to crafting the questionnaire that entails:

- asking the questions in a logical order,
- wording the questions in a way that avoids leading the respondent to answer in a particular way,
- avoiding unfamiliar or ambiguous language and terminology, and
- using scales appropriately.

We'll take up each of these points in turn, briefly, but in enough detail to give you a sense of the intellectual rigor of the work. Keep in mind that entire textbooks have been written on the subject of how to write effective survey questionnaires. Consider the following a basic primer.

RULE 1 – The questionnaire must have a logical order.

All surveys begin with an introduction about the topic and often an explanation of why it is in the respondent's interest to take the survey.

> Welcome to this survey about COMPANY X'S products and services. This survey will help COMPANY X better understand their customers' needs and concerns and be able to respond to them.
>
> Your participation will take just a few minutes of your time, and in return for your help you will receive a $5 gift card. Whether your input is positive or negative, it will be appreciated.
>
> We will ask a number of questions on a variety of topics and will request comments from you. You may not be able to answer every question. It is fine to reply "Not sure" to any question. We appreciate your feedback, but it is not mandatory that you respond.

It is quite common that the survey is not intended for just anyone, but for people who meet certain qualifying characteristics or conditions. Depending on how the respondent answers a set of **screening questions,** he or she may be invited to take the full survey or be politely "terminated."

> When your company makes decisions regarding the selection of group employee benefits, which of the following best describes your role?
>
> 1. Specify/define my company's requirements
> 2. Identify and evaluate alternative providers
> 3. Recommend preferred providers
> 4. Make final purchase decision for the provider
> 5. Own my company's budget
> 6. Evaluate the business impact of the benefits
> 7. None of the above (TERMINATE SCREENER FAIL/SOFT EXIT)
>
> Please tell me approximately how long ago did you make your last purchase from COMPANY X? (READ LIST)
>
> 1. Never (TERMINATE SCREENER FAIL/SOFT EXIT)
> 2. Within the last 3 months
> 3. In the last 4 to 12 months
> 4. More than a year ago (TERMINATE SCREENER FAIL/SOFT EXIT)

Once past the introduction and screening questions, the order of the questions should run from general topics to very specific ones. The following is an example of a survey about a new product idea. The sponsoring company wants to learn how appealing the new product is and the degree to which the company's brand would increase the product's appeal. In such a survey, the flow of questions might be as follows:

1. What similar products the respondent currently buys

2. The frequency of buying these products

3. The brands used

4. What is liked or disliked about these products

5. What, if any, unmet needs does the respondent have in this product category for which a new product might fill the gap

6. A brief description of the new product idea followed by questions regarding what is liked, disliked, level of interest in purchasing such a product

7. A question about whether knowing the product was being introduced by the research sponsor would have any impact on its appeal, and why or why not

8. Basic demographic information about the respondent

There is a "science" behind questionnaire construction, why general questions are asked before very specific ones. You want to ease the respondent into the topic and put the respondent in the right mindset to think seriously about a new idea and respond to questions about it. You also want to avoid sensitizing or biasing the respondent in a way that will influence how he or she might respond to some key questions.

Let me use the example above to explain what I mean by bias. A key question is No. 5, whether the respondent has any unmet needs in the product category. Answers to this question will provide the research sponsor with important information on whether its new product idea is aligned with what consumers are looking for. It's possible that the respondent may identify some ideas the sponsor wasn't aware of. Now if the respondent was asked first about the new product idea and later questioned about unmet needs in the product category, it is quite likely that the product idea could influence the respondent's answer to the needs questions. Specifically, the respondent might list needs suggested by the new product idea that he or she hadn't previously considered.

While we are on the topic of the order of survey questions, let me call your attention to one very important requirement for any customer satisfaction survey. In such surveys, the intent is to find out how satisfied the respondent was with a recent transaction experience (e.g., sought information, bought something, spoke with customer support, etc.), or generally how loyal he or she is to a brand based on any number of experiences. These types of surveys will measure the degree of satisfaction or loyalty and also capture feedback on any number of experiential elements that may impact the respondent's overall sentiment toward the brand. Experiential elements include such issues as how helpful was the company's rep, was the respondent able to obtain what he or she was seeking, how competitive is the brand's price, how helpful is its website, and so forth.

It is absolutely imperative that any satisfaction or loyalty question be asked first, immediately after the introductory commentary and screening questions. This serves two major purposes. First, it captures the respondent's top-of-mind feelings towards the brand. That is what we want to know. If we were to ask the respondent to think about all of the details of his or her experience with the brand first *and then* ask the satisfaction or loyalty question, we have, in short, sensitized the respondent. The second reason is a very practical one. Satisfaction or loyalty studies typically are repeated over time and the results are trended. For various reasons new questions will be inserted into the survey and others removed. Putting the key measures upfront enables the researcher to trend the data over time without there being any effect on the results as a function of having changed the questions.

RULE 2 – Never use "leading" language in writing a survey question.

The goal of market research is to gather and report information about what people think and how they behave with respect to some product, service, or issue. Our task as researchers is to be as unbiased as possible in how we solicit this information. We want the survey respondent to tell us what he or she actually thinks or does, unfiltered by attitudes or social constraints. This in itself

> The KEY LESSON to learn about question ordering is that questions influence one another in terms of how someone may answer them.

is no small task. Psychologists and sociologists have been trying to understand human behavior for hundreds of years. It's as much an art as a science, and we're still a long way from definitive explanations. At the very least, we want to give every survey respondent a blank slate to tell his or her story.

Here is a simple example of a leading and non-leading question:

Leading: *Please tell us **how much you like** this new product by using the scale below.*

Non-Leading: *Please use the scale shown below to tell us **how you feel about** this new product.*

In the "leading" question we are biasing the respondent toward telling us he or she likes the product. The use of the word "feel" in the "non-leading" question is more neutral.

RULE 3A – Use easy-to-understand language.

The respondent has to know exactly what you are asking. There can be no ambiguity. Use simple language and keep questions short. Avoid using words that have ambiguous meaning or terms that may be unfamiliar. It will only confuse the respondent, a sure way to cause him or her to become frustrated and discontinue the survey.

Unfamiliar Terms: *Do you have* **primary fiduciary responsibility** *in your household? (what?????)*

Much Better: *Are you the person in your household* **most responsible for your finances?**

RULE 3B – Be specific and direct about what you are asking.

Non-Specific: *What has your experience been working with our customer service reps?*

More Direct: *How satisfied are you with the ability of our customer service reps to resolve your problem?*

RULE 4 – Use response scales appropriately.

The content of a survey questionnaire consists primarily of **structured questions.** These are very specific questions, each with a range of possible answers provided in the form of a list of multiple choices or a response scale. Everyone is familiar with the list question format—for example, *please tell us what sports you participate in by checking the appropriate answer from the list below.*

But let's take a closer look at response scales, a common type of survey question. The most commonly used response scales are **dichotomous** and **interval**.

A dichotomous scale sets up a straightforward agree/disagree, true/false, either/or, or yes/no choice.

Interval scales are used to measure the strength of your feelings about something or your propensity to behave in a certain way. The interval scale typically consists of 5, 7, or 10 points, the distance between each point presumed to be equal. The most commonly used interval response scale is the **Likert Scale,** which is used in conjunction with a battery of attributes or statements about a product, service, company, or issue. Typical ways in which Likert Scales are used are shown below.

How likely are you to recommend Company X to a friend or colleague?

Not at all Likely									Extremely Likely
1	2	3	4	5	6	7	8	9	10

Please tell us how satisfied you were with Company X's customer service rep on each of the following:

Very Dissatisfied									Extremely Satisfied
1	2	3	4	5	6	7	8	9	10

   a. The rep's ability to answer your questions

   b. The rep's knowledge of the company's products

   c. The rep's professionalism

   d. Etc.

Now we'd like to ask you more about the criteria you use when choosing to do business with a company that provides this type of service. Please rate the following criteria based on how important they are to you.

Not at all Important									Extremely Important
1	2	3	4	5	6	7	8	9	10

   a. The company is priced lower than its competitors.

   b. The company is considered an industry leader.

   c. The company is innovative.

   d. Etc.

When using Likert Scales, the researcher may display the scale in different ways:

Question: *How likely are you to use Product X?*

Anchored at the End Points	Fully Anchored
1 – Very Unlikely	1. Very Unlikely
2	2. Somewhat Unlikely
3	3. Neither Likely Nor Unlikely
4	4. Somewhat Likely
5 – Very Likely	5. Very Likely

Recall that I said that Likert Scales typically use 5, 7, or 10 points. There is no hard-and-fast rule dictating how many scale points to use. There are some simple guidelines, however.

Issue		Number of Points
Response Variance	When using scales, it is desirable to get as much variation in the responses across respondents as possible.	7 or 10 works best.
Presentation	Online surveys have some visual constraints.	7 works better than 10.
Anchoring	It is not necessary to label every scale point.	When using 5 points, however, each should be labeled.

Consistency is important. Try to use the same scale and number of scale points throughout the questionnaire to avoid confusing the respondent.

Before we leave the topic of quantitative research surveys, let's discuss **unstructured** or **open-ended** questions. In this type of survey question the respondent is asked to answer a question in his or her own words (e.g., *What, if anything, could Company X do to improve your experience working with them?*). Open-endeded questions provide rich data insofar as the respondent's answer provides more detail than with a structured question, provides an emotional context (e.g., like/dislike), and often indicates the intensity of that emotion.

Unstructured questions are frequently used as follow-ups to structured questions to ask respondents, for example, why they gave a particular rating. The major drawbacks to using open-ended questions are:

1. they take time to answer, which can limit how many other questions can be asked, and

2. they entail post-survey processing costs because analysts have to create codes for the different ideas or themes mentioned that then can be tallied.

Additional Considerations

I want to call your attention to a couple of additional key points about questionnaires. The first has to do with length. We typically like to ask a lot of questions in a survey. However, time limits how much we can ask. While it is not uncommon for surveys to take 15 to 20 minutes to complete, beyond that we start to push respondents' patience.

Another length-limiting issue has to do with what I'll simply call "trying a respondent's patience."

> **Here's a rule-of-thumb:**
>
> In a given minute, respondents can answer **one** open-ended question and **three** structured questions. So a 15-minute-long interview might consist of about 45 structured questions or a few less if we add in one or two open-ended questions.

Surveys that contain too many repetitive questions (e.g., a question that asks respondents to rate multiple brands on the same lengthy battery of attributes) or an online survey that asks respondents to complete a very detailed matrix of questions can become numbing and cause respondents to abandon the survey.

The final issue about questionnaires is a visual one and pertains to how we present scales. When a survey is administered by an interviewer, such as in a phone survey, we must present the scalar response choices by stating the most positive to the most negative choices. Just the opposite is true for an online survey where the respondent sees the response choices. That's because we remember what we last hear and we read from left to right. We want to avoid biasing respondents to give more positive answers than they might otherwise do. If we have to create a bias, it is better to make it on the negative end of the continuum.

Consider these examples:

Phone Survey

For each of the following services you are currently receiving from Company X, please tell us how satisfied you are by using a scale of 1 to 10 where a "10" means you are extremely satisfied and a "1" means you are extremely dissatisfied.

Online Survey

For each of the following services you are currently receiving from Company X, please tell us how satisfied you are by using the scale shown below.

Very Dissatisfied									Extremely Satisfied
1	2	3	4	5	6	7	8	9	10

The Sample

The subjects of a survey are referred to collectively as the **sample**. The population in question may be very broad, such as all consumers, all adult men, all registered voters, etc. Or it may be some sub-group of interest to the researchers, such as people who own a particular product, live in a particular geographic area, are at a certain income level, are customers of the survey's sponsor, etc. Whether the target population is defined broadly or narrowly, there may be reasons to further subdivide the sample by other relevant characteristics such as demographics (e.g., age, gender, income, education, etc.) or purchase behaviors (e.g., brand usage, heavy vs. light users of a product, etc.).

The ultimate size of the sample is determined largely on the basis of statistical soundness. We can never survey everyone, so we are left to "sample" the population in question. Any estimate of some characteristic of a population (e.g., those interested in a new product idea) expressed as a percentage or a numerical average obtained through a survey is subject to statistical error. Up to a point, the larger the sample, the smaller the error. You have probably read or heard about a public opinion poll in which 1,000 people were asked some questions, and the findings are reported with the disclaimer, "These results are subject to an error of plus or minus 3 percentage points." What that means is that if we actually could survey everyone in the population of interest, the "true number" would be somewhere between plus or minus 3 percentage points of the results obtained by questioning just 1,000 members of that population.

How much error we are willing to tolerate is both a question of statistics and budget. A sample of 100 can have an error range of plus or minus 10 percentage points, whereas the error range associated with a sample of 1,000 is only about 3 percentage points. If possible, both in terms of budget and the population being large enough to find enough people, a good rule of thumb is to sample at least 200 people of any group or sub-group of interest.

> HOW MUCH ERROR we are willing to tolerate is both a question of statistics and budget. A good rule of thumb is to sample at least 200 people of any group or sub-group of interest.

A critical issue associated with survey samples is the question of **representativeness.** Since we can never survey an entire population of interest, it is very important that our sample of that population accurately represents the universe from which it was drawn. We cannot claim, for example, that X% of adults are interested in the product in question if our sample is not reflective of all adults. Achieving a representative sample of some target population requires that two conditions be met. The first is that the researcher has access to contact information (e.g., addresses, phone numbers, email addresses) for every member of the population of interest. The second is to have a means by which to randomly select individuals (that is, choose every *nth* name) from that population.

Meeting these conditions is, in part, a function of how we conduct the survey. The process of sampling reflects methods that have been refined over time in survey research. We turn to that next.

Data Collection Methods

The first scientific surveys were conducted in person by trained interviewers going door-to-door through neighborhoods. Credit George Gallup, who, among others, devised sampling methodology based on U.S. Census information that enabled survey researchers to represent the entire U.S. population or any demographic subgroup of interest with no more than about 1,000 interviews. Such methodology used census tracts (i.e., the smallest territorial unit for which population data information is known) and random selection techniques to determine which individual households would be interviewed. In many cases, additional random selection procedures were used to select the appropriate individual within the selected household. The results produced a sample that reflected the target population at large.

By the 1960s, door-to-door interviewing was rapidly being replaced by telephone interviewing that used **random digit dialing (RDD)** as the means of selecting a representative sample among all households. This method relied on computers to generate random digits that corresponded to telephone numbers. The major advantage of telephone interviewing was the sheer fact that it was much less expensive to conduct than the highly labor-intensive in-person interviewing.

In the 1970s, **computerized telephone interviewing (CATI)** was introduced, creating logistical efficiencies which, in turn, resulted in additional cost savings. Now the sampling and dialing was done in rapid succession by a computer. The computer, however, did not replace the trained interviewer.

By the late 1990s with the growing presence of the Internet and email, market research surveys turned increasingly to **online data**

collection. This methodology offered additional benefits to the researcher: it was even less expensive to conduct than telephone surveys, faster to administer, and enabled the respondent to participate in the survey at his or her convenience. On the other hand, critics were quick to question the representativeness of online survey samples. At first, there was good reason to do so, insofar as the proportion of households with computers and Internet access was relatively low. According to the 2011 U.S. Census, 71.7 percent of all households had Internet access. That still leaves almost one-third of households who would be missed in any online survey. Another concern then and now is that many online surveys use **panels** of people who have agreed to regularly participate in surveys as the **sampling frame.** How representative of the general population are such people? More about this shortly.

A 2014 snapshot of the market research industry shows that many firms continue to do telephone interviewing, particularly when the target population is business employees and email addresses of qualified respondents are not available. In these situations, telephone interviewing may be the only way to contact qualified respondents within the organization because the phone provides a convenient way to screen for the desired respondent by job title or job function. The interviewer simply asks to speak to the person who is responsible for decisions regarding the purchase of the product or service in question and is directed to that individual.

Online surveys continue to be the dominant mode of data collection. However, the platform for responding to these surveys is quickly migrating from desktop computers to smartphones and tablet devices. The latter provide a way to catch people closer in time to events that may be the subject of the research—for instance, having just finished a retail transaction or having just seen a product display in a store. The one drawback with mobile surveys is brevity. They must be kept relatively short—under 10 minutes compared with 20+ minutes via desktop computer and telephone surveys. In addition there are some constraints in what can easily be seen on a smartphone versus a desktop computer. We will return to mobile surveys later.

Statistically Sound Samples

The more rigorous data collection modes of door-to-door and CATI interviewing facilitated the use of scientific sampling techniques to achieve sample representativeness. In moving to surveys delivered via the Internet, we have traded sampling rigor for logistical and financial benefits. Statistics, however, enables us to right our wrongs to some degree. If we know the demographic breakdown of our target population, we can weight our survey data to correct for any disproportionate outcomes. For example, let's say we have conducted a survey with a sample of 1,000 adults of whom 55 percent were male and 45 percent were female. We know from Census data, however, that males represent 48 percent of the population. So our sample is over-represented by males and under-represented by females. We then weight the survey results to correct for this situation, thus bringing our sample back in line with the population we are representing.

> A NAGGING QUESTION of market research surveys: do the people who cooperate actually represent the continuum of psychological constructs that are associated with any survey topic?

While this step addresses any demographic aberrations in our survey sample, there remains the question of whether any sample represents all points of view on the subject. There always has been a nagging question in market research surveys—namely, do the people who cooperate actually represent the continuum of psychological constructs (e.g., attitudes, behaviors, perceptions, wants, etc.) that are associated with any survey topic? A commonly voiced criticism is that only those who have an extreme point-of-view (e.g., love the product or hate the product) bother to complete a survey. While this bias may be inherent in many surveys, we have considerable proof to suggest otherwise on the basis of surveys that have accurately predicted future market behavior.

Here again, we have statistical tools that enable us to adjust survey samples to "iron out" any non-demographic aberrations in our sample. One such technique is called **propensity weighting.** We insert into a survey a short battery of questions where the results are already known. Such questions might relate to beverage preferences, media habits, or physical activities. This technique was used widely when Internet surveys first became popular to address the concern that those who participated in such surveys were not representative of the population at large.

Interpreting the Data

The last step in the survey process is to interpret the data. The research analyst's first task is to tabulate the data into what are called **banner tables** (see page 116). The typical survey will have two or three banners that present the data first by all respondents (i.e., Total), then by any number of desired subgroups of respondents. A subgroup may be defined in terms of a demographic characteristic (e.g., gender, age, income, education, race), an attitude (e.g., positive or negative towards the product or issue), or a behavior (e.g., user or non-user of the product category).

With the tabulated data in hand, the research analyst then presents the results for each question in the form of an understand-at-a-glance graphical chart that will be used in the report to follow.

Example: Customer Service – Relative Impact of Performance Attributes

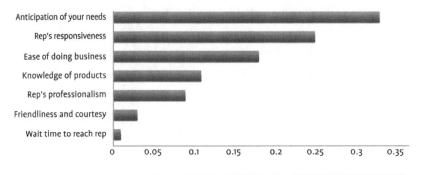

The Research Report

Once the data have been displayed visually, the analyst's next task is to package the results in a written document that typically follows this outline:

- Background and objectives of the research
- Methodology used
- Executive summary of key takeaways, conclusions, and recommendations
- Detailed findings
- Appendix material (e.g., profile of respondents, explanation of methodology)

It is not the goal of this book to explain the how-to's of writing a solid, comprehensive research report, but there are a few key points to remember:

- Answer each objective of the research.
- Avoid telling the reader what he or she can see. Don't just repeat the numbers and percentages in paragraph form; use the data to tell a story.
- Be more visual and less wordy.

Let's take a look at each of these.

Answer each objective of the research.

Every research study sets out to answer one or more BIG questions:

- How loyal are our customers?
- How interested are people in buying our product?
- Who are the best prospects for our service?
- Are people aware of our advertising?
- How is our company perceived in the marketplace?
- What do people think are the most important issues, for example, facing Congress?

The answers to these questions are the focus of the research report. For each of these over-arching questions the survey has posed 10, 20, or 40 questions or more. Accordingly, the report needs to weave together the answers to the supporting questions to provide insights into the BIG questions. These insights are delivered in the Executive Summary section of the report. In market research, just as in journalism, you want to state the headline first and then back it up with relevant details.

EXAMPLE: Executive Summary

Customer loyalty towards Company X, as measured by the concept of Commitment, is strong. Over half of those surveyed can be classified as committed to the company. Other manifestations of customer loyalty are reflected in the high scores Company X receives on the measures of overall satisfaction, likelihood to continue doing business, and likelihood to recommend. The value of committed customers is reflected in the fact that they are shown to be far more likely to recommend Company X and express the intention of continuing to work with the company than those whose bond with the company is weaker.

Avoid telling what can be readily seen—tell a story.

When asked to write commentary based on sets of data, newcomers to the market research industry often fall into the trap of simply restating what the reader can readily see in the graphs and charts. What the analyst needs to do is help the reader quickly extract meaning from the data. Here are two examples of my point—one wrong and one right.

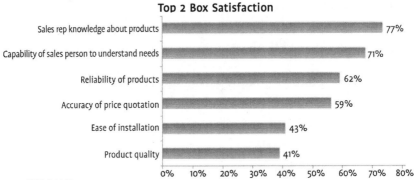

WRONG

Seventy-seven percent of the respondents are very satisfied with the *sales rep's knowledge about products*, and 71 percent are satisfied with the *sales rep's ability to understand needs*, and 62 percent are satisfied with the *reliability of the products*.

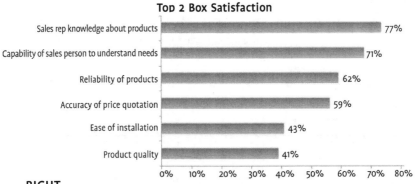

RIGHT

The company is shown to be doing a very good job of meeting customer expectations with respect to the performance of its customer-facing staff. On the other hand, the company is under-performing in its customers' eyes with respect to its products.

Be more visual than wordy.

Remember the old adage a picture is worth a thousand words? This truism is particularly relevant to market research where so often large amounts of data or a complex idea can be conveyed quickly and efficiently with just a single careful-ly-crafted image. Today's research reports often tell the story not with page after page of charts and verbiage but with ex-pertly designed infographics. The major

> It is the job of the analyst to help the reader QUICKLY EXTRACT MEANING from the data.

market research firms often employ graphic artists who work with analysts and project managers to translate and summarize the find-ings of a research study into attractive, easy-to-digest "posters" that can be inserted into the final report.

The following is an example:

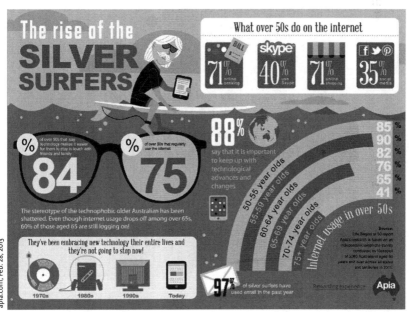

"Visualization enables a non-linear way of analyzing informa-tion where one can first see the shape of the story, understand patterns and relationships, and then only look into meaningful components to provide recommendations in real time. This enhanced capability presents a change on how we communicate today in corporate settings. Storytellers will be able to display and interpret data movements and answer questions on-the-fly rather than take additional time to perform data cuts."

—Ruben Alcaraz, *Data Visualization–*
The New Art of Understanding,
GreenBook blog post, September 17, 2013

CHAPTER 5

The Market Research Process: An Overview

In the last chapter I introduced the different tasks inherent in any market research study. In this chapter we will broaden our lens and talk about the entire process—from what prompts the need for a research project, to how a company is selected to undertake the project, to the design and execution of the project, to delivery of the results.

From Request for Proposal (RFP) to Deliverables

It is a rare company that does not contract for at least one research project per year to help address some important marketing issue. The very largest companies spend millions of dollars a year on market research and usually have a fairly well-defined research agenda from year to year. These firms are likely to have one or more research studies running at all times to assess their customer loyalty and the degree to which they are meeting customers' expectations following various transactions (e.g., sales, support, billing, etc.). Customer loyalty studies are typically done annually, and customer satisfaction studies are done on an ongoing basis. Such companies are likely to be doing concurrent research to track how their brand is perceived. Research dollars also will be spent in support of new products and services and their advertising.

Smaller organizations, on the other hand, may spend only thousands of dollars and approach market research on an as-needed basis. The request to "research the issue" usually comes from the company's marketing or sales departments. If the need is for research in support of the company's reputation among diverse stakeholders (e.g., customers, investors, regulators, the media, etc.), the initiative may come from the PR department, or from the HR department if the request is to assess employee engagement.

Since it is the rare organization that has its own resources to design, field, and report on a market research study, the company will most likely turn to external market research suppliers for help. Those companies that routinely commission market research projects usually have a small "stable" of preferred research partners (i.e., vendors) to whom they turn. Others may consult colleagues for recommendations or go online to industry sources such as the Green Book, a well-respected source for finding research suppliers.

A company putting out a **request for proposal (RFP)** will usually send it to three or four market research suppliers. However, it is not unusual, especially among companies who do little research, to send the request to as many as a dozen suppliers. Twice I found out that I had won a project 14 companies had bid on!

The RFP

In the RFP, which may run from a few pages to dozens, the company will provide an overview of itself and a detailed description of the market research project it is seeking to do. In this description, the company will articulate the following:

- The **Business Questions** to be answered.

These may include such questions as:

~ How loyal are our customers?

~ What is our image vis-à-vis our competitors?

~ What are the desired features and functions of our product concept?

~ Which of a set of advertisements best communicates the value of our product?

- The **Specific Objectives**
This section will list very specific questions or directions within the larger topic. For a study about customer loyalty, for example, the specific objectives may instruct the research supplier to track loyalty over time, identify how loyalty differs across different sub-segments of customers, identify which aspects of the customer experience (e.g., sales, support, communications, etc.) drives loyalty.

- **Survey Design Specifications**
At a minimum, this section of the RFP will provide the research company with the basic information it needs to construct a budget. This will include information on what populations (e.g., current customers, former customers, different demographic groups, etc.) are to be surveyed, the preferred mode of data collection (i.e., online, phone, in-person), and the desired number of surveys. Other pertinent information might be included:

~ Languages other than English, if the research is to be done in multiple countries

~ The use of some desired metric (e.g., *Net Promoter Score*)

~ How the results are to be shown (e.g., by different demographic groups)

~ Specific deliverables such as data tabulations, electronic data files, reporting format

~ Timing of the research

~ Budget

- **Decision Criteria for Selecting a Supplier**

  Here the company requesting proposals will spell out the basis on which they will select a winning proposal. In no particular order, this will usually consist of knowledge of the company's industry and issues, relevant experience, the quality of the proposal in addressing the objectives, and price.

- The **Deliverables**

  This is a list of what the company expects the research company to provide them *at a minimum*. Typically this will include:

  ~ A report

  ~ The raw data

  ~ A presentation

The research suppliers typically will have two to three weeks to prepare and submit their response to the request, which will take the form of a proposal. During this time they will be allowed to ask questions about the RFP.

The Proposal

 Game on! The solicitation for market research is essentially a contest where winner takes all. For the market research firms receiving the request, the challenge is to figure out how to beat out all those other suppliers. Winning is rarely about being the lowest bidder. More often it is about having the **smartest** and most **engaging** offer. Let's explore this a bit.

The proposal is where you, as the research supplier, must **sell** your firm to the company requesting the research. The operative word in that sentence is "sell." For many people entering the field of market research, selling is an anathema. People who feel comfortable around statistics and research designs are not by nature people who like to sell anything to anyone. I'll discuss this issue later when we look at the different job roles in market research. For now, however, there is a need to sell the proposal, albeit mostly via the written word and visual graphics.

> WINNING is rarely about being the cheapest. More often it is about having the SMARTEST and MOST ENGAGING offer.

There is certainly no single formula for writing the smartest proposal, but there are certainly a number of key steps and underlying fundamentals. Let's explore these.

Step One: Make Personal Contact

Once the RFP is in hand, the research supplier will assemble a small team to respond. Each member will have one or more key roles to play—methodologist, lead author, budgeter, client relationship manager. The team members may or may not have had some prior contact with the client about the RFP. However, even if you feel the RFP contains everything you need to know to put together a solid proposal, it is mandatory that you have a follow-up phone call or in-person discussion with the client in order to establish a personal dialogue. Most RFPs, no matter how well-written, will leave the reader with questions. An

> An unstated decision criterion in selecting a research partner is always INTERPERSONAL CHEMISTRY.

unstated decision criterion in selecting a research partner is always interpersonal chemistry—"Do I want to work with these people?" Accordingly, it is imperative that you establish an interpersonal connection. It also gives you further opportunity to create a favorable impression of your team's qualifications for undertaking the work.

Companies who buy market research differ in terms of how closely they will let their suppliers approach when it comes to RFPs and proposals. Unfortunately, there are many companies who treat the

RFP process as a very formal procedure. Their protocol may dictate not allowing the supplier to talk to the company researchers, requiring that all questions be submitted through a procurement officer. This is the least desirable scenario since it's the job of the procurement officer to act as a non-informative gatekeeper.

Step Two: Writing the Proposal

There are several fundamentals involved in writing an engaging proposal.

> "The two most engaging powers of an author are to make new things familiar, familiar things new."
>
> —William Makepeace Thackeray

1. Know your client.

Your conversations with the soliciting company and your proposal must show that you have at minimum a fundamental knowledge of their business, their industry, and their challenges. A familiarity with the company's website is essential. Most of what you will need to know will be found there. You also should bring to bear any other knowledge that you may have about this company and its industry, based on other relevant experience you and your colleagues have had.

Convey this knowledge in both a direct and indirect fashion. You don't need to go overboard telling the client all about his or her business. They already know more than you do. One or two paragraphs may suffice to convey that you are familiar with the basics. Use the client's logo on the cover of the proposal to show that you have taken the time to look at the company website.

2. Organize the proposal in a logical way.

There is no one single way to write a proposal. Occasionally the client may dictate a format, but it is usually left up to the proposing firm. I tend to favor the following outline shown as a series of Power-Point slides:

- A brief **introduction** in which you thank the client organization for inviting your firm to respond, followed by a short statement about the purpose of the request.

Overview of Our Proposal

Thank you for inviting us to submit our proposal to conduct your **Consumer Experience Study.**

We recognize how important this market intelligence is for Company X, and we will work with you in a collaborative manner to ensure that your business objectives are completely met. Through this engagement our focus will be on delivering accurate and actionable information in a timely manner. We are confident that our experience and subject matter expertise is unmatched by our competitors and result in valuable strategic and tactical guidance.

Elements of the Proposal:

1. The business need
2. What success looks like
3. Our value
4. Our approach
5. Schedule
6. Budget
7. Appendix

Our proposal provides detail on our point-of-view and recommended methodology for addressing the requirement discussed in your RFP.

Please consider this a working-document which we will modify as warranted based on our subsequent dialog.

- The **business need** that prompts this request for research. In this section you articulate the client's key business questions and what they will learn from doing the research.

The Business Need

COMPANY X understands that success In today's marketplace requlres that customers' expectations be met at every touchpoint.

Accomplishing this requires that the company have a comprehensive understanding of the customer experience and expectations. With this insight the company will be in an optimal position to deliver experiences that will delight customers, while ensuring that the company is neither over- or under-delivering these experiences.

With this in mind, COMPANY X requires a comprehensive quantitative study that will define the customers' expectations at each key touchpoint and how customers currently rate COMPANY X on these touchpoints.

KEY AREAS OF UNDERSTANDING

What do customers want In terms of the medium and performance standards?

Where are we over- or under-delivering against our customers' expectations?

Will customers pay for a premium experience?

How do we align our human and technical resources against customers' expectations?

- **A look ahead to the benefits.** Take your readers to the end: What will a **successful research engagement produce?** Tell them what success looks like. This reinforces the rationale for doing the research and shows that you have the big picture in mind.

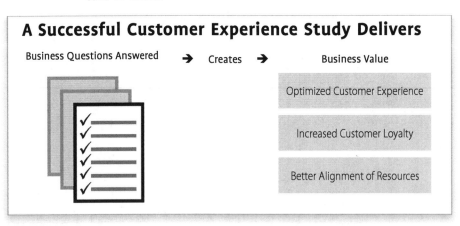

A Successful Customer Experience Study Delivers

Business Questions Answered ➔ Creates ➔ Business Value

Optimized Customer Experience

Increased Customer Loyalty

Better Alignment of Resources

- **Why your firm?** Unless there is an existing relationship between the client and the proposing firm, it is important to state briefly what differentiates your team from the competition, what value your company brings to this research project. If you feel more information about your firm is needed, put it in the Appendix. The client doesn't want to read endless self-promoting material.

What Differentiates Us

- We know your industry having conducted research and consulting on behalf of 12 of its top 20 firms.
- We are recognized as thought leaders on Customer Experience Management.
- The insights we deliver will be highly actionable and tied to bottom-line outcomes.
- All of the resources needed to undertake this engagement are in-house.
- We will assign a dedicated team of highly experienced researchers and consultants to this engagement.
- Oversight will be provided by a member of our executive team.

- **Your approach** to addressing the client's information needs. In the next series of slides you lay out your proposed methodology, timeline, and budget. Starting with your recommended methodology, talk about the sample design, the types of questions that will be posed, how the data will be collected, and how you plan to analyze and report the information. Be as specific as possible so the reader walks away with a clear understanding of what you plan to do and, more to the point, why. Perhaps the most important part of this section is the analyses you plan to use and how these analyses will answer the client's questions. This is where you can show your smarts and even differentiate yourself from the competition.

3. Frame your recommendations conceptually.

I have written and read hundreds of proposals in my career. The dumbest and least engaging are those that merely spell out the mechanics of the proposal:

> We will do 500 telephone interviews with individuals who meet the screening criteria for the survey. The interview will take 15 minutes and pose questions that answer your objectives. We will provide the results in a written report, blah, blah, blah . . .

Most, but not all, of the issues that we address in market research lend themselves well to a conceptual discussion that provides a sound framework for why you are proposing a particular methodology. Consider for a moment the topic of customer loyalty. Prior to launching into a detailed discussion about the questions we will ask and the analytics we will use, I like to talk first about the *concept* of customer loyalty. For example, I might discuss the value of having loyal customers. We know for a fact that loyal customers are a profitable asset for any company. They don't leave you, they spend more with you, and they advocate on your behalf. From here I may talk about how customer loyalty can be viewed in terms of a relationship that exists between the company or brand and its customers. Moreover, this relationship has two dimensions. The first is *rational*. This is where the company or brand is meeting its customers' basic needs—the right portfolio of offerings, competitive prices, etc. The second is *emotional*. This is where the company or brand has earned the customer's trust; the company makes customers feel that it is looking out for them, values them, and has their best interests in mind.

> Provide a CONCEPTUAL FRAMEWORK that will substantiate the types of questions you propose asking and the analytics you will use to make your proposal stand out as thoughtful and smart.

Finally, I may go on to say how important it is for organizations today to view their customers in terms of a relationship and to foster this bond as a means of differentiating themselves in an otherwise commoditized marketplace. It's always a good idea to provide a conceptual framework that will substantiate the types of questions you propose asking and the analytics you will use. It makes your proposal stand out as thoughtful and smart. You want your reader to think, "These guys know their business. I just learned something I didn't know."

4. Tell the reader how you will answer their business questions.

A smart, winning proposal does more than simply go through a lengthy description of the questions you will ask and analyses you will do. It will tie the discussion to the big business questions during the RFP. Specifically, you want to tell the reader how each line of questioning you propose and each type of analysis you plan to do actually answers the business questions. Here's a graphic example of what I mean:

> Our client has asked us to submit a proposal to measure customer loyalty. One of the desired outcomes of the research is to find out where, if at all, the client may have to make changes in the customer experience to increase customer loyalty. Typically this involves asking respondents to indicate their level of loyalty to the company and then rate their satisfaction on any number of relevant **touchpoints** they routinely experience (e.g., *sales, support, billing, etc.*) and their perception of company attributes (e.g., *product quality, innovation, industry leadership, etc.*). We use standard statistical regression techniques to show us the relationship between touchpoint satisfaction and company perceptions vis-à-vis customer loyalty and in so doing can identify the relative impact each touchpoint and perception attribute has on "driving" customer loyalty.

We then can plot the results to easily show our client where change may be warranted.

Action Grid
Identifying and Prioritizing Key Drivers

We call this an **action grid.** The horizontal axis represents the average satisfaction scores provided by the survey respondents for each of the touchpoints and company attributes of interest. The vertical axis plots these same items in terms of their impact on the loyalty measure as derived from the regression analysis. As such, it offers a simple way to identify opportunities and priorities for improving loyalty. Items that fall into the *Primary Strengths* quadrant mean that they have the most impact on customer loyalty and the company is perceived to be doing well. Accordingly, the client should keep doing whatever they are doing and talk about it in their communications to their customers. Items that fall into the *Action Items* quadrant also have the most impact on customer loyalty, but the company is underperforming in its customers' eyes. These are the things that the company should pay attention to and improve. The *Monitor* and *Secondary Strengths* quadrants contain items that have relatively little impact on customer loyalty, so they do not demand immediate attention.

In the example above, we see that *Customer Support* has the biggest impact on customer loyalty by virtue of being at the top of the grid. What this means is that for every unit increase in customer satisfaction scores for this touchpoint, the customer loyalty measure will increase the most. We also see that *Customer Support* receives relatively lower satisfaction scores by virtue of being on the left of the grid (i.e., in the *Action Items* quadrant). At the same time, we see, for example, that *Prices* also receives relatively lower customer satisfaction scores. However, its impact on customer loyalty is shown to be somewhat less (i.e., in the *Monitor* quadrant) than that for *Customer Support*.

From this simple visual we are able to answer our client's question regarding where to focus their efforts to improve customer loyalty. The answer is to concentrate on improving customers' perceptions of how they do support. This will do more to improve customer satisfaction and loyalty than any changes they make regarding their pricing.

5. Be reader-friendly.

Demonstrating your smarts in a proposal is also about knowing how to deliver the message. The last thing you want to do is bore your readers or lose them in myriad verbiage and figures. Research proposals take various forms—from simple letter documents to more formal Word documents to graphics-driven PowerPoint documents. Irrespective of the form used, any proposal should be concise, logically organized, relatively short, free of jargon and unfamiliar terminology, and visually appealing. I favor PowerPoint proposals in which compelling visuals can take the place of lengthy passages of text. Compare the following:

EXAMPLE 1

Boring:

The questionnaire will cover the following issues:

- Awareness of brands
- Desired characteristics
- Brand usage
- Demographics
- Familiarity with brands
- Perceptions of brands on these characteristics
- Likelihood of switching and why

More Interesting:

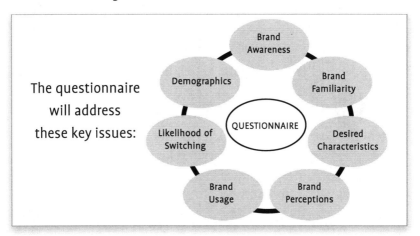

EXAMPLE 2

Boring:

By way of summary, the survey will encompass the following:

- A total of 1,200 consumers will be surveyed nationally.
- The survey sample will be representative of the U.S. in terms of key demographics.
- The survey will be approximately 20 minutes long.
- The target audience will be adults 18 years or older living throughout the U.S.
- The survey will be done online.

More Interesting:

Survey Specifications

 Online Survey   1,200 Consumers   Representative of U.S. Adults 18+ Years   20 Minutes

---

You can give your PowerPoint proposal a crisp, contemporary look by using icon images in place of photographic images. Suppose that somewhere within the proposal you talk about meeting with your client to discuss the findings of your research. You may want to illustrate this activity.

So 20th Century	*21st Century*

Step Three: The Follow-up.

Once the proposal is submitted you need to follow-up with the client within a few days to confirm that he or she has received your proposal and to solicit comments and questions. Here again companies differ with respect to how they handle this phase of the research request. Ideally, you will have an opportunity to meet with the client and present your proposal. You may be given an hour to present, followed by a question-and-answer session with an assembled body of internal stakeholders (e.g., one or more people from market research, internal clients who will use the information, a representative from purchasing). I always found these experiences to be especially exciting and occasionally scary. This is where you really have the best opportunity to sell your company and your approach.

Within a week or two you will be notified of the company's decision. Some of the most exciting words to hear, either via email or on the phone are "I'm pleased to tell you that we have selected your company to undertake the NAME OF PROJECT." Of corse, the message can just as likely be one you'll come to dread: "After careful consideration we have decided to award NAME OF PROJECT to another firm."

The Project

 Congratulations! If you are on the supplier-side you have won the project, and now you have to get going. If you are the research buyer you will not have too much to do until the project is complete. You will spend most of your time upfront with your supplier and internal clients discussing the questionnaire content. It is a crucial task insofar as the research will be only as good as the questions that are asked. The supplier and buyer will go back and forth numerous times from rough drafts to final wordsmithing.

Once the questionnaire content is finalized, it will be programmed for either telephone or online administration. Data collection typically will take two to three weeks, followed by the cleaning and tabulating of the data, also two weeks. Figure another two weeks for analysis, which may involve advanced statistical procedures, and yet another two weeks for reporting. All in all, most surveys take 10 to 16 weeks to complete from kick-off meetings to final deliverables (e.g. data file, data tabulations, report).

The last step in the research process is to present the report. Typically, a **preliminary report** is sent to the client for their review. At this point it is considered a draft and changes may be made based upon the client's review. Once researcher and client agree on the content, the report is given a final formatting and findings are presented to internal stakeholders. This may be done in person or via an online conference.

While the report presentation is usually the end of the project, there may be an opportunity for the research team to take one more step with the client in the form of a **workshop with internal stakeholders**. Here the idea is to help the client digest the results, disseminate them, and act on them. The typical workshop may run a half-day or a full day and involve 10 to 15 participants who represent different functional areas of the company (e.g., sales, marketing, customer experience). The role of the researcher is to facilitate the internal dialogue. Such a workshop provides the research organization an opportunity to demonstrate its additional value as business consultants. Often such a workshop can lead to a request for additional research.

CHAPTER 6

Application of Market Research to Business Issues

In Chapter 1 we learned that market research is used to help organizations answer key business questions and, in so doing, make better decisions. We touched on the four basic questions that market research is designed to address. Now we'll explore how the research is used to help make those decisions.

Let's start with a list of some of the most common business questions:

- What are the unmet needs of the buyers of my product?
- What features or functions should we add to our new product?
- How should we position our service to be most appealing to potential customers?
- Are we meeting the expectations of our customers when they interact with us?

The best decisions are informed decisions. The role of market research is to **inform** the decision, never to be the sole source for the answer. The ultimate answer to any business question has too many variables to be reliably supplied by any one source, be it a research study or something else. In all my years in the market research Industry I rarely, if ever, encountered a client who expected a research study to answer every question. The experienced buyer of research knows that any one piece of research can address only a narrow aspect of his or her business case. The following is an example of how one company used market research to help inform its plans to offer a new consumer service.

CASE STUDY 1
Assess Our Value Proposition

An online retailer had achieved success as a leading provider of party goods. The company decided to enhance its services by offering a party-planning consultancy. In so doing they saw an opportunity to differentiate themselves from their competitors by offering a more customer-centric service. They commissioned a market research study among consumers who have purchased party goods from either brick-and-mortar or online retailers to answer the following business questions:

- Identify the degree to which current party goods retailers were meeting consumers' requirements and expectations.
- Identify unmet needs.
- Gauge reaction to their party planning service concept.

The research was done in two phases. In the initial qualitative phase, an online discussion (via a *Bulletin Board*, a type of online focus group) was conducted over several days with 25 randomly selected consumers who responded to questions posed by a moderator. To participate, responders had to meet the following criteria:

- Age 19–62
- Two-thirds female, one-third male
- Have made at least one purchase from an online, catalog, or brick-and-mortar party goods retailer in the past 3 months

The goal of this first phase was to identify consumers' needs and pain points regarding the purchase of party goods. The deliverables were a set of hypotheses regarding:

- Consumers' requirements and expectations regarding the purchase of party goods
- Consumers' actual experiences
- The *ideal* experience
- Initial reaction to the client organization's proposed service
- Likelihood of using the proposed party planning service

This research provided both a set of hypotheses to be tested in a follow-up quantitative survey, as well as the basis for the types of questions to be posed.

In Phase 2, an online survey was conducted among 1,003 representative consumers drawn from an online consumer research panel who met the following criteria:

- At least 18 years old
- Two-thirds female, one-third male
- Household income of $35K+
- Have made at least one purchase from an online, catalog, or brick and mortar party goods retailer in the past 3 months

In a survey that took approximately 10 minutes to complete, the hypotheses generated in the initial qualitative research were quantified.

The research revealed that the client's proposed service met important consumer needs. Specifically, it aligned well with the relative importance many consumers place on being able to create unique and entertaining parties for friends and family.

This basic two-phase research study provided the client with critical fundamental information—that consumers experience certain pain points with respect to party planning and that the client's proposed service appeared to do a good job of handling these discomforts. This was enough to give the client a green light to keep going, but it did not, nor was it intended to, answer every question the client had regarding how to successfully take this service to market. Details related to the service's features, website functionality, and pricing, as well as how the company would attract customers to the service, would be answered later, perhaps after further research.

CASE STUDY 2
Re-engineer Customer Touchpoints

In the first case study we saw how market research was used to inform a company's introduction of a new service offering by answering some basic strategic questions. Sometimes, the questions are quite tactical (e.g., What price do we charge? What name do we give this product? In what size do we package the product?). In the following case, we will see how a technology company used market research to "re-engineer" its customer service from the perspective of customer expectations.

The technology company needed to improve the entire customer service experience. In an online survey lasting 25 minutes, which included a sophisticated decision-modeling exercise, 1,200 technology decision-makers in small businesses answered questions that provided input into how they specifically wanted to experience each of the following:

- How long they were willing to wait on "hold" for technical support
- Their preferred window of time for a technical support appointment
- How frequently the company provided them with a status update on technical support work
- How long they were willing to give the company to complete the technical support work
- How long they were willing to wait for the company to respond to an email request

As a result of this research, the company realized that its customers' expectations were often different from the company's internal view of same and so redefined many of its expected performance indices. In some cases the company was over-delivering to customers' expectations. They also stopped spending hundreds of thousands of dollars on undesired customer experiences.

CASE STUDY 3
Strengthen the Relationship with Customers

For the past 10 years this Fortune 500 manufacturing company has made customer service paramount in its business value proposition. The company's mantra is *Customer First*. This message starts at the top of the company and pervades every aspect of the business, especially every way it touches its customers. Every year it fields a massive global survey among customers in over 35 countries, involving more than two dozen languages, to find out how well it is meeting customers' expectations across every key interaction.

The research has enabled the company to obtain a hard measure of its customers' loyalty and the relative impact that key aspects of the customer experience (e.g., sales, support, communications, training, etc.) have on this bond. Moreover, it gains insight into where changes in processes or communications may be needed in order to overcome any weaknesses in the customer relationship.

Managers in each country and operating division review the research findings and conclusions and are directed to develop action plans to address any critical issues. These in turn are reviewed by senior executives who hold these managers accountable for the required actions and subsequent results.

CASE STUDY 4
Avoid Trying to Be All Things to All Constituents

It is a well-understood marketing axiom that there is no such thing as a homogeneous customer base nor an *average customer*. Therefore, treating all customers the same will result in over-delivering experiences to many, while under-delivering to others. Catering to "the average" results in operational inefficiencies and has a negative impact on the organization's bottom line. This is a common problem for any organization, for-profit or not-for-profit.

Market segmentation is a major area of work within the market research Industry. At some point in time, most large organizations attempt to segment their constituents in ways that go beyond simple demographic characteristics or behaviors. It entails some of the more sophisticated types of analyses used by researchers. It also tends to be some of the most expensive research undertaken by organizations. The goal of this type of research is to understand how one's constituents group themselves in multi-dimensional ways— how they think, how they behave, and what they look like. When done well, this type of research provides robust information to guide marketers in targeting and messaging to desired audiences in ways that will resonate with each subgroup targeted. In short, it enables the company to better target its customers and avoid inefficiencies.

One of the largest professional associations recognized the value of market segmentation and commissioned a research project to segment its membership. The purpose was to better understand differences across members and how to tailor its offerings to the different segments. Like all associations, it was faced with two key problems: how to get members to engage more with the organization, and how to target younger professionals to replace its aging membership. More than 5,000 of its members in the U.S. were surveyed. They answered questions about their reasons for affiliating with the professional association, whether and how they engage with the organization, their attitudes toward the association's programs and services and the like.

The research identified six key member segments, each with somewhat distinct needs, wants, behaviors, and characteristics. One such segment was a surrogate for the young professionals. With this information, the association was able to fine-tune its programs and marketing to each segment, as well as understand better how to attract new younger members.

CASE STUDY 5
Protect Brand Value

One of the keys to succeeding in business is to be able to differentiate your product or service from that of your competition. This is becoming increasingly difficult as products, services, and prices are becoming increasingly commoditized. A large industrial company with products and technology central to the construction of manufacturing plants sought to pre-empt further commoditization by taking actions to differentiate itself in order to be requested to bid more often on new construction projects.

The company undertook qualitative research to complement existing insights obtained from quantitative research in order to represent the full value chain and identify patterns of influence. Accordingly, it commissioned in-depth interviews among developers, consultants, and original equipment manufacturers. Through this research, the company's management was able to understand:

- The most efficient strategies for impacting the business, including where to target efforts
- The role of product brand and component brand in the overall offer—and when in the process it matters
- The context for marketing communications and sales teams
- Emerging trends that they could take advantage of.

CASE STUDY 6
Ensure Product Appeal

History shows that few successful product launches achieved their ultimate success without having at least some market research done to guide the birthing process. This is not to say that market research always ensures that the product will be a success. The history of market research has its fair share of "horror stories" of products that failed, despite what the market research suggested would happen. In the 1950s Ford introduced its Edsel model to much fanfare and much failure. It continues to stand today as one of the auto industry's biggest failures. The Edsel failed for lots of reasons (e.g., internal work force issues, an economic recession) that had nothing to do with the quality of the research done.

Herein lies an important point. The predictive power of market research is limited by many factors. One key factor is that it takes a "the world as it exists today" perspective. A second key factor is that it cannot feasibly take into account external phenomena like an economic recession or corporate workforce problems. Accordingly, while consumers may have expressed very positive reactions to the car in Ford's pre-launch surveys, there was no way to account for the external factors that led to the car's demise.

Leaping from mid-twentieth century autos to modern cruise ships, the number of major builders of modern cruise ships is small and most are forever locked in an intense competition to win orders from the world's cruise ship lines. One of these manufacturers needed to understand the appeal of its newest design vis-à-vis those of two key competitors. A market research study was conducted in which cruise ship passengers in three world cities were exposed to three "unbranded" cruise ship concepts and the researchers used Discrete Choice Modeling to present varying cruise ship attributes.

Before I tell you how this turned out for the company sponsoring the research, a brief description of Discrete Choice Modeling is warranted. One of the primary pursuits of market research throughout its history has been to understand and model how people make decisions. A considerable amount of groundbreaking work was done in the 1960s and 1970s by industry giants like Rich Johnson, Yoram Wind, and Paul Green to develop methodologies that would enable the researcher to get inside the consumer's head and understand how he or she makes decisions. Their work was based on the basic fundamental fact that consumer decisions involve trade-offs—what are people willing to give up in order to get something of more value to them. It is rare that we can have everything we want. Real-life decision-making involves choosing among options with varying mixes of strengths and weaknesses. The resulting methodologies are based on the psychological theory of **utility maximization.** According to this theory, consumers select the alternative that yields the greatest total utility for them.

Discrete Choice Modeling (DCM) is one such methodology that asks survey respondents to do realistic tasks, as if they were actually making decisions on the product or service category in question. In the DCM task respondents are shown three or more product or service profiles defined in terms of a number of key attributes at varying levels or options, instead of being asked to evaluate one product or service profile at a time. The alternative profiles shown to respondents may be just the client's offering (a representative slice of the market) or they may include the competition's offering, thus representing the market as a whole. DCM results are shown as market shares.

The following is an example of a typical DCM task.

Survey Support

If you were presented with these options on a typical eating out occasion, which one would you choose? You may choose "None" if you would not choose any of the options.

Cuisine Type	Chinese	Indian	American	
Distance	<5 minutes away	<10 minutes away	<15 minutes away	None
Rating	★ ★ ★	★ ★ ★	★ ★ ★	
Price	$$	$$	$$$	
	●	●	●	●

CONTINUE

The respondents for the cruise ship study were American and European regular travelers on cruise ships. They were recruited using both in-person and telephone methods and were able to complete the surveys by themselves, with the aid of an in-person interviewer or at a central interviewing facility. The results of the DCM simulations demonstrated that one ship design was clearly preferred to other designs. The results were used to support the marketing of the new ship and the ship manufacturer's public relations efforts. The new ship design ultimately won wide acceptance in the marketplace.

CASE STUDY 7
Identify the Optimal Pricing Structure

DCM is widely used in pricing studies to identify the optimal pricing of a product or service. A large bank was rethinking its fees to its business customers. Different plans were being considered involving minimum balances, checking fees, access to different types and levels of information, and set fees for other types of business financial services. The bank was seeking to evaluate different pricing structures as well as determine what value customers placed on certain features of the plans. Their ultimate goal was to increase revenue by driving customer activity and offering plans that would have lower attrition.

To address these requirements, research was undertaken among the bank's current customers using DCM methodology. Several different pricing structures were tested, along with a series of current and potential service features.

Using an Excel simulator, individual level DCM results were linked with stated usage intent from the study and historical banking activity. The findings helped the client project preferences for different plan configurations as well as the revenue associated with the plans.

CASE STUDY 8
Inform a B2B Distribution Channel Strategy

This case illustrates how initial qualitative research is often used to develop hypotheses that are then tested in a follow-up quantitative survey. A supplier of construction materials needed to understand its customer needs and purchasing behavior across various product material categories in order to reshape its market positioning and distribution strategies. In particular, the company needed to know how various distribution channels complemented one another to best effect.

Targets for the research were customers purchasing across several product categories and via a range of different channels. The research involved two phases. The first employed qualitative group discussions to identify the key decision-making criteria and explore the broad associations between the different products. In a follow-up survey, these findings were then "quantified" with a larger sample of customers.

The research was able to characterize the strengths and weaknesses of the client's respective distribution channels for different product categories and identify what changes in business strategy would minimize overlap in the sales effort and ensure that each channel was targeting customers with a competitive offering.

Does This Kind of Work Intrigue You?

If you like the prospect of working in close collaboration with colleagues and strategic marketers in various industries to design research studies that provide insights like these, then you will find the job of market research analyst engaging, intellectually stimulating, and professionally satisfying. It's especially satisfying when you see your research findings implemented and have the chance to develop long-term relationships with clients who've come to rely on your contributions and insights.

CHAPTER 7

The Future of Market Research

The market research industry has changed dramatically since I entered the field in 1970. These changes cover the full spectrum of how we design surveys to how we collect, analyze, and report survey data. The players themselves have changed in terms of their numbers, nature, and culture. While the future of the industry is still to be written, the seeds of change are quite evident. Here is a list of some of the major factors that have transformed the industry and will continue to have huge impacts going forward.

- Technology for capturing and reporting data
- Big Data
- Neuroscience
- Social Media

Let's take a look at each of these.

Technology for Capturing and Reporting Data

The biggest changes have occurred with respect to how we collect and report data. In the late 1990s the Internet was the industry game changer as online surveys became the primary mode of gathering opinions. The Internet continues to be the engine of change.

 **Mobile** is the current hot topic. Most people in the developed world now own one or more mobile devices. Mobile phone penetration stands at an estimated 96 percent globally (International Tele-communication Union, February 2013). Ownership of tablets is also growing at an exponential rate. In vast developing markets like China, India, and Brazil, more people have access to a mobile device than to a landline phone. Moreover, mobile devices are rapidly becoming the preferred platform for accessing the Internet. For those who want to understand millennials, mobile technology may be the only way to go.

For some time now, the marketplace has been pushing market researchers to conduct more surveys via mobile devices than through other traditional modes of data collection. This has tremendous implications for the look and length of surveys. Because we rely so heavily on mobile devices to gather information and communicate with others, our attention spans are much shorter than they used to be. Moreover, there is only so much visual material one can squeeze onto a small screen. On mobile devices question content must be minimized and surveys should never take longer than six to seven minutes to complete.

Survey design issues aside, mobile technology gives us the ability to capture consumer feedback in real time following a transaction or exposure to some stimuli (e.g., an advertisement, a display, a purchase, etc.). GPS technologies can pinpoint a consumer's location and send him or her a short survey as he or she leaves a store or stands in front of a product display. Mobile technology also is opening the door to new kinds of data collection. Consumers are now being asked to take photos of what is in their shopping baskets or make a video as they use a product.

Quirk's Marketing Research Review (August 2014) asked Bob Pankauskas, Director of Consumer Insights at Allstate Insurance, about his company's use of mobile technology for market research.

"It's only a matter of time before we migrate all of our research platforms to mobile devices. We want our respondents to be able to choose when, how and where they answer our questions. There are incremental opportunities that mobile provides—being in the moment, getting a real-time view of sponsored events and just the ability to capture insights when customers are in the midst of an experience. We're also really excited to utilize consumer-generated images to get more color and context from mobile cameras and not just words and numbers."

Finally, while mobile technology has given market researchers a gold mine of new data gathering opportunities, it also is creating potential land mines with respect to privacy concerns. Increasingly, we are sharing more information about our lives that, in turn, can be readily shared with other parties such as credit agencies, police, the media, etc. unbeknownst to us.

> While MOBILE TECHNOLOGY has given market researchers a gold mine of new data gathering opportunities, it also is creating potential land mines with respect to privacy concerns.

When I came into the industry I spent hours and hours reading and coding stacks and stacks of written responses to open-ended survey questions (e.g., "Why did you say you would be unlikely to buy brand X?"). I then had to sort these surveys into piles, each pile reflecting a different answer category. Then I assigned a code to each category for purposes of tabulation. Talk about tedious work!

Fast forward a few decades. Computer software called **text analytics** has replaced the human coder. Responses to open-ended survey questions are scanned for themes and the positive/negative/neutral sentiments behind those themes. The software also can tabulate and graph this information. It's a powerful tool for mining large amounts of verbatim data, and we will undoubtedly continue to see advances in this technology in the years ahead.

Far too many trees have been lost to countless written market research reports. While there always will be a spot for the written report, the executives who order research today have little time to read through voluminous tomes. Moreover, they are usually looking for some key metrics or brief, clear answers to the business questions that prompted the research. Today we're able to use **electronic desktop reporting solutions** to put the data on the executive's desktop with user-friendly graphics and controls. This technology too will continue to keep pace with demand and eventually make written reports seem archaic.

One such version of the desktop data portal, **Enterprise Feedback Management (EFM)** systems, has been a complete game changer for conducting customer satisfaction surveys following a transaction. An online survey invitation is sent to a consumer immediately following a transaction (e.g., returned a rental car, checked out of a hotel, purchased a meal, etc.). Such surveys usually consist of just a few questions: satisfaction with the experience, likelihood of recommending the business to a friend or colleague, reasons for rating. Upon completing the survey, the results are captured and tabulated and a report is sent to a manager at the client organization. If the respondent voiced a complaint, the manager also may get an action alert to call the customer and address the problem.

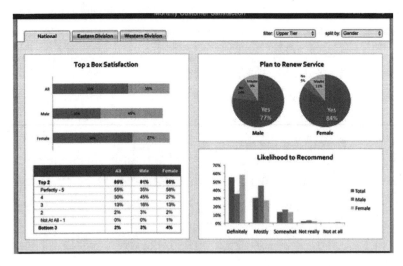

Hertz Rent-a-Car uses an EFM solution to assess its customers' satisfaction with their rental experiences. I frequently rent Hertz cars during my business travel. After one such incidence, I returned my car to the Hertz facility at the Denver airport and the next day received an online survey from the company. As usual, the first question asked was "How likely are you to recommend Hertz to a friend or colleague?" The scale ran from 0 ("I definitely would not") to 10 ("I definitely will"). I answered with a 0—not because I had had a bad experience but because I simply don't go around recommending rental car companies to friends and colleagues. The truth is, I always rent from Hertz. Within an hour of hitting the "send" button on the survey, I was contacted by phone by the Hertz manager at the airport. He asked how Hertz had failed to satisfy me. I explained my answer and reassured him of my loyalty to Hertz. He thanked me.

It's a good example of how this type of solution is used to both conduct market research and manage the customer relationship. It's also an example of how surveys sometimes fail to measure what they are intended to measure. In this case, Hertz took my response as an indication of my lack of loyalty, when the just the opposite was true.

Big Data

David Brooks, the *New York Times* op-ed columnist, wrote, "over the past few centuries, there have been many efforts to come up with methods to help predict human behavior—what Leon Wieseltier of **The New Republic** calls mathematizing the subjective. The current one is the effort to understand the world by using **Big Data**."*

---

* *New York Times*, April 15, 2013

Vast amounts of data travel across the Internet every second. Big Data is the term for how we move, capture, analyze, and report large, fast-moving, complex data sets. A 2013 survey by Gartner, a major information technology research and advisory company, reported that two-thirds of those companies polled planned to make major investments in Big Data technology.

Why all the interest in Big Data? For starters, it's available, so why not look at it? Large databases have always had a place alongside market surveys to provide, among other things, context and perspective for what people report. What is changing, however, is the extent to which we increasingly rely on ever-larger data sets from which to observe and predict human behavior. Despite all of the advancements in the social sciences and market research, we still struggle to really understand human behavior, let alone predict how people might behave in the future.

Big Data is already playing a major role and will become increasingly important to society in general and market research in particular in the years ahead. There are both positive and negative aspects to Big Data. Let's turn first to some of the negatives.

> BIG DATA is the term for how we move, capture, analyze, and report large, fast-moving complex data sets.

Big Data is very good at showing us patterns of human behavior, but we don't yet have reliable insights into how two or more behaviors are linked by cause and effect. Herein lies the problem: We are tempted to draw correlations between two sets of data without verifiable insight into causality. Let's consider an example. Imagine you are an analyst sifting through available data on automotive purchases. You notice that sales of luxury cars have shown a recent increase of 12 percent. At the same time you are looking at data on home sales and notice a similar uptick in the sales of expensive homes during this same time frame. You wonder if there is something about buying an expensive car that causes people to also purchase a home or vice versa. But there is no way to answer that question from these two data sets. We do know that luxury cars and expensive homes both cost money, so if sales of each are rising simultaneously a more likely explanation might involve a third factor—income—which may or may not have shown any changes during the time period in question. At the moment this is the problem with Big Data: the data reveals patterns which may be valuable in their own right, but we cannot attribute causality. The core problem is that there is not anything intrinsic to Big Data that lends itself to understanding the patterns seen. You can look 100 times for the relationship between two things and you are likely, just by chance, to find five false correlations.

Another issue with Big Data is that the tools used to analyze it can be gamed. A frequently cited example of this is automated programs used to grade student essays. Such programs often rely on measures of word length and word sophistication, both of which have been shown to correlate with how humans grade the same essays. Students find this out and intentionally start writing longer (not necessarily better) sentences and using bigger (not always appropriate) words, rather than actually learning how to write a better-constructed and better-reasoned essay.

The other issue with Big Data is the question of privacy. So much is now known about each of us from sources such as our shopping behaviors, online search behaviors, and financial records. Accordingly, there are increasing calls for restricting what data can be collected and how it can be used, in order to protect consumers' privacy as well as prevent the misuse of personal data. The latter speaks again to how Big Data can be misinterpreted. Consider this example. You are doing online research for an academic paper on risky behaviors. Over a week you spend several hours looking at sites about sky diving, mountain climbing, motorcycle racing, and the like. A data miner somewhere tracking your click stream might interpret this behavior as an indicator that you are an extremely risk-prone person. This information then finds its way into life insurers' databases erroneously marking you as a poor candidate for insurance!

Okay, enough about the negative side of Big Data. Let's look at some of the positives. For starters the focus on correlations when analyzing Big Data is not all bad. In a 2014 article about Big Data in the *New York Times*, the author, Sendhill Mullainathan, made the following point about correlations: "Correlations are what motivate us to look further. If all that Big Data does—and it surely does more—is to point out interesting correlations whose fundamental reasons we unpack in other ways, that already has immense value."*

Big Data provides valuable information where traditional surveys fail. Market research is always asking what people are doing and why they are doing it. People are better at explaining their behavior than they are at accurately recalling it. Big Data provides us with the "what" they are doing, while surveys give us the "why."

A 2011 study by the *MIT Sloan Management Review* and the IBM Institute for Business Value reported that companies that analyze the Big Data available to them outperform their industry competitors. In short, Big Data enables companies, especially those in retail or service industries, to tailor offers and experiences to their customers based on the knowledge of their customers' actual behavior.

Finally, the value of Big Data is in a business' ability to mine and analyze it. For those considering a career in market research, this is the giant new horizon that will open the door to many new and exciting jobs.

Neuroscience

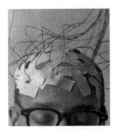

If people were completely rational and capable of articulating why they do what they do, we could continue just asking our survey questions. Unfortunately, we are neither rational nor creatures of habit, governed by past learning. What we did

---

* "Hold the Phone: A Big Data Connundrum," *New York Times*, July 26, 2014.

yesterday is not very predictive of what we will do tomorrow. We are ambivalent, ambiguous, self-deceiving, forever changing. We also frequently filter what we say in a survey. We may give socially desirable answers to a live interviewer, answers that do not accurately reflect who we really are. Or we may respond in ways that reflect how we would like others to see us, answers that may or may not reflect our actual opinions or behaviors.

Recognizing this predicament, market research professionals have made great strides in how we ask questions to get at the underlying truth. At the same time, psychologists have been working for decades on how to bypass the questionnaire altogether and discover what makes people tick by looking inside their minds. The work of Nobel prize–winner Daniel Kahneman has provided valuable new thinking on this topic. In his 2011 best-selling book, *Thinking, Fast and Slow,* Kahneman, a neuro-economist and psychologist at Princeton University, laid out a construct of how people process their environment. *System 1* pertains to our unconscious, emotional responses to stimuli and *System 2* pertains to our more rational, cognitive responses. Traditional market research methodologies enable us to tap into *System 2.* We need the tools

> PSYCHOLOGISTS have been working for decades on how to bypass the questionnaire altogether and discover what makes people tick by looking inside their minds.

provided by neuroscience, however, to tap into *System 1.* It is for this reason that many especially large research companies use both methodologies and will argue that both should be used in studying certain consumer issues. One such area has been advertising research.

As far back as 1970 when I entered the market research industry, we were using **galvanic skin response (GSR)** and eye movement to gauge consumers' reactions to advertisements. The GSR is a way to measure the electrical conductivity of the skin, a function of skin moisture created by sweat. The degree to which we sweat is controlled by our sympathetic nervous system. The idea is that skin moisture can be an indication of our psychological arousal. Imagine sitting in a lab with a cuff on your arm, its wires running to a machine recording the electrical current passing through your skin. All the while you are being shown a series of different ads for a product. The GSR methodology records a physiological response to what you are looking at. It cannot tell us if your aroused response is positive or negative; some questioning is still required.

Yet another methodology involved recording eye movement across an advertisement or product concept. A variation of this measured **pupil dilation,** the idea being that pupil dilation indicated heightened focus.

Eye movement continues to be a valid channel of investigation. However, the GSR has been largely replaced by more modern methods such as **magnetic resonance imaging (MRI)** of brain functions and **electromyography** to measure facial muscles for positive and negative reactions to stimuli. Psychologists have made great leaps in using MRI technology to map how the brain responds to different stimuli. Electromyography involves hooking electrodes to the zygomatic muscle around the mouth (used for smiling) and the corrugators muscle in the brow (used for frowning). Advertising researchers have been quick to latch onto these advanced measurement techniques and use them to detect emotional reactions to marketing materials (e.g., print ads, commercials, direct mail pieces). Such technologies enhance our ability to understand which aspects (e.g., visual, auditory) of these marketing stimuli elicit various positive and negative reactions in consumers.

Like Big Data, neuroscience data is not readily interpretable. Remember the earlier case study about market segmentation where I noted "there is no such thing as an average customer"? Well, people also differ with respect to how they physically respond to the same test stimuli.

The use of neuroscience in marketing research is still in its infancy. Advancements in this area will surely be exciting, ensuring its place in the market researcher's tool bag. In an article on the state of neuroscience and market research for *Marketing Daily*, Elisa Moses, EVP of Neuroscience and Emotion at research giant Ipsos, said the following: "The reason traditional market research firms offer neuro tools is simply that *most studies are better off with them*. Moreover, clients have become more savvy, and now request them. As the realization sinks in, researchers cannot continue to address only the rational, conscious side of reaction or the emotional, visceral side. Both are critically important."*

Social Media

There are over 1 billion active users of Facebook. Millions of people use Twitter, LinkedIn, offer their comments on business websites, and use countless other social media channels. In short, there are vast amounts of discoverable data out there in the form of online chatter, and marketers are trying to get their heads around how to mine it and use it to their advantage. At the very least, every major corporation has staffers looking online for what people are saying about the company. Progressive companies also are actively engaging with customers and prospective customers through social media. It is a rare business that doesn't have a Facebook page or doesn't interact online with its constituents, answering questions and promoting its products and services.

What is still missing at this writing is any sophisticated effort to quantify and analyze all of this chatter. Harris Interactive made an attempt around 2009 to harness social media. The idea was to empanel enough people who would allow the company to follow them on Facebook, Twitter, and other social media sites. By so doing the

---

* "The State of Neuroscience in Market Research," *Marketing Daily*, June 14, 2013.

company could tell its clients not only *what people were saying* about them but *who was saying what.* It was an ambitious project that barely got off the ground because Harris Interactive found it impossible to recruit enough people to make the program viable. In order to find enough comments about any one brand, the panel needed thousands and thousands of people likely to be talking about that brand. Without widespread opting-in by consumers, it was never possible to identify a specific brand and tell the brand managers who was saying what about the company in social media.

It's possible that we may never actually arrive at a valid way to quantify social media. Rather, its use in market research will be as an adjunct to other data sets (e.g., surveys, Big Data, etc.). What we will develop are ways of looking at data from multiple sources and the tools to synthesize all of it to provide some degree of insight. Let's just say that social media is and will continue to be an area that captures the creative attention of market research methodologists. Stay tuned.

The Future Is Integration

Leading industry experts see the near-future of market research as involving not one form of data versus the other, but rather the *integration* of disparate data (e.g., surveys, social media, behavioral Big Data, etc.). The problem always has been that no one source of information tells the entire story. We can survey people to ask what they think and why, but the self-reporting tends to be inaccurate. Behavioral data captured at supermarket checkouts or via monitors on our devices provides hard evidence of what we are doing, but not why. Increasingly, researchers will be

> Leading industry experts see the near-future of market research as involving not one form of data versus the other, but rather the INTEGRATION of disparate data (e.g., surveys, social media, behavioral Big Data, etc.).

tapping all these different data streams simultaneously to draw more comprehensive and conclusive pictures of what people are doing and why they are doing it.

This in turn has tremendous implications for what the market research function will become and the types of people who perform these tasks. More about this in Part 2.

The field of market research, like just about everything else in the world today, is changing rapidly. The implication for those entering the field is clear: you have to be prepared for change and willing to embrace it. Those who are flexible and fast on their feet will succeed. Those who don't will be left behind.

PART 2

Market Research as a Career

"To find a career to which you are adapted by nature, and then to work hard at it, is about as near to a formula for success and happiness as the world provides. One of the fortunate aspects of this formula is that, granted the right career has been found, the hard work takes care of itself. Then hard work is not hard work at all."

—Mark Sullivan

CHAPTER 8

The Players:
Buyers and Doers

 The world of market research and those who work in the field can be divided into two camps—buyers of research (clients) and those who sell or do research. To the chagrin of most people in the second camp, buyers or clients refer to them as vendors, a word that has a somewhat pejorative connotation, at least to everyone I know on the doer side.

The majority of market research professionals will go through their careers in one camp or the other. Not many people work both sides of the market research business. There is a reason for this. Those who choose the client side are expected to be well-versed in market research methodologies, but they rarely get very involved in actually designing, fielding, analyzing, and reporting a survey project. Their role is to serve as ombudsmen between the information needs of their internal clients (e.g., marketing, sales, PR departments) and the external research companies who do the work on their behalf. In this role, they become very good at understanding their industry as well as the demands, idiosyncrasies, politics, and culture of their organizations. On the other hand, they lack the experience that comes with actually doing the market research.

Let's say you choose the supplier or vendor side and go to work for a market research company. Over time you will become well-versed in how to do all the tasks associated with the design and delivery of a market research study. You will probably learn something about many different industries, but not enough about any one industry to be thought of as an industry expert. Some people do, of course, make a career of specializing in one or two industries. What these folks lack, however, is the experience of navigating the cultural and political labyrinth of most big businesses. In short, when it comes to hiring across the client-supplier divide, each side lacks what the other wants most.

There are other reasons why most people stay on one side of the fence or the other. Many people on the client side find a market research job in a corporation to be a great stepping-stone into other departments (e.g., marketing) and levels (e.g., management). In fact, their end goal may never have been to become a life-long market researcher. On the supplier side, many market researchers come to enjoy the hands-on experiences associated with the research process and like having the chance to experience a broad variety of marketing issues and industries over time. Let's take a closer look at each camp.

> When it comes to HIRING across the client-supplier divide, each side lacks what the other wants most.

The Buyer Side

Most large businesses have a market research department or at least a dedicated market research person. Some of the very largest corporations like General Motors, Microsoft, and Bank of America have scores of dedicated market research staffers. Again, their job is to take the needs of the internal stakeholders whom they support and translate these into requests for proposals. They help decide which research supplier to hire and then oversee the work. Upon completion of the research, they may write their own report from the information provided or package it into sub-reports for different internal constituencies.

What Is the Role of the Corporate Market Researcher?

The client-side market research job is very different from the supplier-side. Sue Morgenstern has spent more than 20 years in market research for a telecommunications giant we will call Z.

I sat down with her to discuss the role of the corporate market research person. A transcript of that discussion appears below.

Q: Sue, how would you describe your role as a market research manager at Z?

A: I serve as the liaison between internal marketing managers and market research suppliers.

Q: How do your internal clients view that function?

A: That depends on the client. Sometimes my colleagues and I are in the position of needing to justify our value to certain internal clients who may fancy themselves to be market research experts. Sometimes senior management within the company attaches little value to market research. The corporate culture can vary from company to company and can change suddenly when there's a turnover in senior leadership. When IBM was in the business of making personal computers, it employed many people to conduct research in support of their product design and marketing efforts. By contrast, Steve Jobs of Apple never believed in the value of market research.

Q: Does Z's market research department ever set the research agenda?

A: That depends on who controls the market research budget. Some time ago our department had a large budget and spent it on research we felt would benefit the company, even if no one in marketing had requested it. Today virtually all of the research dollars at Z are owned by internal clients who have very specific research requests. However, we are not just order-takers. Our internal clients take our advice on how best to execute the research they request.

Q: Do you and your colleagues have a line of sight into what research will be done over the year or is it more ad hoc?

A: I would say it's ad hoc. The only research we know about in advance are a couple of tracking studies that get repeated year after year.

Q: What should someone know when taking a client-side market research job?

A: Ten years ago the biggest difference was that the client job was easier than that of the supplier. We used to be able to keep standard business hours and could leave work at five. This has changed. The internal pace has picked up considerably as technology has shortened timeframes. Everything has to happen quickly.

Ben Tolchinsky has been in the market research industry for many years on both sides of the fence. He currently is with a leading communications company in its Consumer Insights group. Asked to describe the differences between a client-side role versus supplier-side, Ben told me, "They are very different, almost like night and day. The role that supplier research plays in a decision is relatively small. It is one input along with many. Knowing how to maximize the value and meaning of the research—not only what is communicated, but how it's communicated and to whom—is a key part of the corporate role. Effectiveness on the corporate side of the business is as much or more about strategic consulting and organizational knowledge as it is about research quality." On the issue of how much input his department has in setting his company's research agenda, Ben said, "At times, the Consumer Insights department is an influencer, and at times it is an order-taker. Being an order-taker is not always negative, and we do not always have visibility into the strategic decisions being considered throughout the organization. Even as an order-taker, we still have the opportunity to influence and lead. Often times, organization politics play a role, and we have to decide which battles are worth fighting."

Jun Gao works for a global healthcare company. His title is Senior Manager, Sales & Marketing Analytics. Jun had this to say about the differences between a client-side research role versus supplier-side: "The client-side role has more direct impact on one particular company's operations from various angles. The supplier-side role provides expert level guidance to many companies in a few focused fields like advertising testing." When asked what he would tell someone who wanted to go into market research, Jun said this: "On either the client side or the supplier side, getting consulting experience along with the hardcore market research skills will be the best way to grow in this field."

A client-side job requires that you know not only about market research but also about your particular industry. Industry knowledge is something you can and will learn on the job. Over the course of a career, you will probably find yourself gaining expertise across many very different industries.

People working on the client side often stress the need to be diplomatic. This is a requisite no matter what department you work in. While all organizations involve internal politics, it's usually a greater factor on the client side than on the supplier side because most client organizations tend to be more hierarchical than the typical market research agency. Diplomacy can take many forms. At one organization, I've heard it said that it was politically incorrect to say anything negative about anything at any level. At this organization, internal researchers sometimes have to put a positive spin on research that may not support the internal client's idea.

Onward and Upward

Can a job in the market research department lead to a bigger role in the company or elsewhere? In many organizations a research job can indeed be a stepping stone. A researcher operates from a unique platform from which you can see the breadth of the company's business and where it is heading. You are likely to be exposed to each of your company's four marketing P's: product, place, price, and promotion. The goal is to put the right product in the right place, at the right price, at the right time.

If not a stepping stone to a bigger job in your current company, market research can give you a solid foundation for a bigger job in another company. The experience of Lakshmi Sundar, currently Senior Director, Marketing Services at Bracco Diagnostics, shows a typical career trajectory.

> "I started my career in market research and spent many years working in a number of different industries. My market research roles in these companies focused on both consumer and B2B environments. I worked on research projects that spanned a gamut of methodologies and scope. The foundation provided by market

research to 'see patterns/trends in data' and 'weave and tell a story effectively' have helped me grow my career in a variety of areas including Information Technology, Commercial Operations, Public Relations, and Social Media Marketing. In fact, I would say a solid foundation in market research is a building block for a career in today's hottest space—Big Data!"

—Lakshmi Sundar, Sr. Director, Marketing Services,
Bracco Diagnostics

The Seller Side

The market research industry has been a vital contributor to business strategy for almost a century. During this time the industry has experienced an explosion of growth in terms of the number of companies that sell research services, and in more recent years, a consolidation among the very largest firms. My career always has been on the seller side, and I have personally witnessed a good deal of this growth and consolidation. The late 1990s and early 2000s saw something of a Pac Man mentality among the industry giants. Some examples:

Taylor Nelson merged with Sofres to become TNS, which was then bought by the Kantar Group. Market Facts was bought by Synovate, which was later bought by Ipsos. Gordon Black bought the Lou Harris company, Total Research, and Yankelovich and became Harris Interactive, which was later bought by Nielsen.

What remains today are a small number of billion dollar global behemoths (e.g., Nielsen, Kantar Group, Ipsos, GfK), a handful of hundred plus million dollar giants (Maritz, ORC, Burke), and thousands of small boutiques and solo practitioners. The 25 largest research companies accounted for 58 percent of the global spending on market research, according to

> Over the past century the market research industry has experienced EXPLOSIVE GROWTH and in more recent years significant CONSOLIDATION among the very largest firms.

the industry publication *The Honomichl 25* (August 2012).

Within the industry are firms that have the expertise to address any marketing issue, do both qualitative and quantitative studies, and are sometimes referred to as "full service." Other firms have deep knowledge in certain industries and can best be categorized as niche players. Indeed, some companies make a specialty of focusing on only one industry. This is particularly true in the healthcare space where the specialization often goes even further, with some companies focusing particularly on pharmaceuticals and others concentrating on medical devices. That's because pharmaceutical and medical device companies like their research suppliers to have a deep and specific knowledge of their business issues and jargon.

Market research companies can also be sorted into those who do only qualitative research versus quantitative research. This is particularly true of the very small boutique outfits and solo practitioners who specialize in conducting focus groups and in-depth interviews.

> The research company side provides you with an opportunity to develop and practice the science and art of marketing research ... there is NO BETTER PLACE to start and learn your craft.

Another subset of businesses serve the other players within the market research industry. These firms may sell survey samples (e.g., online panels, e-mail addresses, lists of names with phone contacts, etc.). Others provide what are called "field services," consisting of telephone interviewing and face-to-face interview services.

Which side of the market research industry fence you land on is your choice, albeit the job market at any particular time may lead you to one side or the other. Industry veteran, Jim Donius, who has spent many years working for both market research buyers and sellers, has this advice for those getting started: "The research company side provides you with the opportunity to develop and practice the science and art of marketing research. Your work is the company's offering and there is no better place to start and learn your craft. The supplier and client sides provide you an opportunity to apply your knowledge to improving decisions, reducing risks, and identifying opportunities. Both offer meaningful career opportunities. You will learn your craft, however, on the supplier side."

Alison Bushell, a colleague of mine at Harris Interactive, spent a dozen years on both the supplier side and client side in market research. Her experience on the client side was with companies in the energy, health insurance, and consumer package goods industries. When asked which side she preferred, she replied "The supplier side indeed. The client-side culture seems to be much less friendly, often counterproductive with lots of evidence of back-stabbing and 'stepping over dead bodies.' Staff on the agency side is more likely to rally behind a common goal, embrace innovation, and focus on excellence—with more teamwork thrown in."

Who Is Hiring?

Trade-offs aside, anyone looking to get into the industry or make a move wants to know where the jobs are. The answer, of course, will vary year to year. In 2014, the hiring picture looked positive. In a report titled "State of the Research Job Market, Spring 2014" (*Marketing News*, April 2014), Karla Ahearn and Naomi Keller reported that the market research job market was looking healthy, as the world economies were recovering. They noted a sense of urgency among those hiring, as reflected in candidates going off the market more quickly. They saw the most robust hiring on the client side, particularly in the pharmaceutical, technology, and retail industries. They also noted that research buyers were looking for more senior-level hires to fill roles on expanding internal market insights teams. This is good news for junior- and mid-level candidates who will be needed to fill those growing departments, as well as back-fill positions as more experienced researchers move up.

If you think that the client side is where you want to be, I suggest you look again at where the research dollars are being spent by industry on page 19 in chapter 3. It's a good starting point.

If you think the supplier side best suits your interests, a useful starting point is to consider which firms employ the greatest number of people.

Top Global Market Research Companies

1. Nielsen
2. Kantar
3. Ipsos SA
4. GfK SE
5. IMS Health
6. Information Resources Inc.
7. INTAGE, Inc.
8. Westat
9. NPD Group
10. comScore Inc.
11. Video Research Ltd
12. IBOPE Group
13. ICF International
14. J.D. Power & Associates
15. Macromill Inc.
16. Maritz Research
17. Abt SRBI
18. Symphony Health Solutions
19. Lieberman Research Worldwide
20. Mediametrie
21. Nikkei Research Inc.
22. ORC International
23. YouGov Plc

Source: ESOMAR Top 25 Global Research Organisations 2012. Note that two companies—Arbitron (originally #9) and Harris Interactive (originally #20) were subsequently acquired by Nielsen.

CHAPTER 9

Why Choose Market Research?

 What constitutes an "exciting job" let alone an exciting career is of course a personal matter. Some find fulfillment commuting to an office five days a week and sitting behind a desk, while others may crave doing tough, physical work outdoors. Assuming you are closer to the first type of person than the second, what is it about market research that attracts new recruits?

If you are like most young aspiring professionals you probably have no idea, and furthermore, may even suspect just the opposite is true. "How can questionnaires and statistics be exciting?" you wonder. Bor-ing!

Well, here's a well-kept secret: market research is about human behavior, and that's anything but boring. It's about thinking conceptually, about thinking strategically. It's also about how to just plain think. It's about unraveling puzzles. It's about informing major decisions that affect the fortunes of companies and organizations, and in so doing affect our daily lives. It's about playing a key role in developing the next must-have digital device, the next-generation airplane, the next Starbucks. It's also is a wonderful training ground for anyone whose ultimate goal is a successful career in marketing.

What was that about "unraveling puzzles?" Imagine you are looking at scores of disparate pieces of information. Your task is to find and tell the "story" hidden in those pieces, a story that is going to answer someone's extremely important business question.

I said that all of this is a well-kept secret because, frankly, the market research industry has not done a particularly good job of promoting itself to aspiring young people. *Quirk's Marketing Review*, a major market research industry publication, reported the findings of a 2013 survey of 1,800 college graduates around the world about attractive career choices. Market research didn't make the top 10 list, and only 13 percent said they would consider it.

Consider my efforts in this book to be one small step in rectifying this situation.

Respect and Value

The work done by market researchers is highly valued by those who commission it. Early in my career I was hired by Market Facts, one of the major market research firms throughout the 20th century (later acquired by Synovate, which was later purchased by Ipsos). I was asked to be lead researcher on a major contract Market Facts had with the U.S. Department of Defense. The project involved surveying over 10,000 men and women ages 18 to 24 about their educational and career aspirations and the likelihood they would consider the military as a starting point. This bi-annual survey was a source of major market intelligence used by all branches of the military to shape their marketing communications and job offerings directed at potential new recruits.

While the project kept me knee-deep in numbers, the excitement for me was the face-to-face interactions I had with my clients. I'll never forget the first time I flew from Chicago, where I was based, to Washington, D.C. picked up a taxi at National [now Reagan] Airport, and said to the driver, "Take me to the Pentagon." Actually I learned soon enough that going to the Pentagon is not such a heady experience, that it's a major waypoint for Metropolitan D.C. buses and subways. In other words, anyone can go there.

Nevertheless, on a regular basis I would meet with civilian and senior military staff to discuss the findings, conclusions, and implications of the study. Many times I was the featured speaker before an assembled group of high-ranking military officers over whom I held command, if only for a few moments. In some related work, I had the opportunity to spend time at West Point, the U.S. Army military academy, where through the market research process, I worked with the academy's leadership and staff to help the corps of cadets (students) become more comfortable with the increasing presence of women and minorities among their ranks. Having cadets call me sir was a bit much, albeit fun. More exciting was my chance to play a small, but important, role in helping to shape the recruiting agenda in the relatively new all-volunteer forces, as well as deal with some serious social issues.

Fast forward some years. I now find myself sitting in conference rooms of some of the most well-known companies in the world (e.g., IBM, GE, Johnson & Johnson, Xerox, MasterCard, Verizon, AT&T, Microsoft), discussing their biggest marketing challenges. In fact, I'm one of the people to whom they are turning for help. You have to be pretty jaded not to consider that an exceedingly interesting, even exciting workday.

Show Your Smarts

Your job in market research will involve working in a team. Sometimes you might be a contributor, other times the team leader. Your role may be that of a generalist or someone who is providing very specific input to the process, such as a statistician interpreting the results of a data model. At every turn, you will have a chance to demonstrate your brainpower and learn from others.

David Smallen was a colleague of mine at Harris Interactive and Nielsen. David has worked on both the client side and supplier side. Much of his career has been in the role of senior marketing scientist (i.e., senior statistician). This is how David sees it:

> "The marketing science professional is the best team member to discuss with the client the links between the client's objectives and the research results that will meet those objectives.
>
> "He or she is responsible for the end-to-end knowledge concerning research/survey design, questionnaire design, survey sampling, issues concerning fielding the survey, data preparation once fielding is done, analytics, and interpretation. Most importantly, he or she is responsible for the integration of all these steps. For example, making sure the questionnaire is designed in such a way that the data will be appropriate for the intended analysis and will meet the client objectives. Because of his or her broad-based knowledge of research design, analysis, and application, the marketing scientist is often involved in the research sales process, both in terms of sales presentations and written proposals.
>
> "Finally, the research scientist acts as a teacher, both for his or her company and client companies. He or she is often called upon to deliver seminars or papers at conferences to discuss the latest research techniques and applications."
>
> —David Smallen, VP, Group Client Director, Analytics, Nielsen

Market research provides an excellent platform for collaborating with a group of smart people to develop innovative ideas and approaches. This function is referred to as **thought leadership**.

One of my colleagues related how he steered his team through a lengthy proposal development process in which they devised an innovative way to measure the drivers of customer loyalty and retention and link them to business processes and financial outcomes. The proposal won his firm a significant research contract with a major international chemical company. It was a particular point of pride for this researcher because on the strength of its innovative approach his firm beat out several other highly regarded international marketing research firms for the business. The research

> MARKET RESEARCH provides an excellent platform for collaborating with a group of smart people to develop innovative ideas and approaches.

process he and his team developed proved to be extremely effective in getting to the root of the issues at hand and was subsequently recognized as a global best practice.

Early in my career, I had the opportunity to be part of a team that developed a groundbreaking methodology for capturing and modeling decision-making. This occurred when I was at Market Facts in the early 1980s. We had a contract with the U.S. Department of Defense to design and field a survey to define the optimal configuration of benefits that the military could offer members of the Reserves and National Guard. Our leader was Rich Johnson who was an analytical giant in the industry and who later went on to create Sawtooth, a leading software company for modeling consumer decision making. The methodology we used was called **conjoint analysis** which is based on the idea that people's decisions involve trade-offs—we give up something of lower value to us for something of higher value. The methodology involved presenting survey respondents with an experimentally determined series of paired choices—*would you prefer to have $2,000 to use for college tuition or two fewer weekends of training a year?*

What was groundbreaking for the time was that we did this "online." We did not have the Internet yet, but we presented the survey to respondents on a device that looked like a big TV set (called a CRT for Cathode Ray Tube) connected by a landline telephone to a central mainframe computer. Various forms of conjoint analysis done through online surveys are widely used today to model how people make decisions.

Stretch Your Mind

As we've seen, market research can help businesses answer major strategic and tactical questions. At the heart of these questions are issues associated with understanding and sometimes predicting human behavior. As a market researcher your job will be to answer these questions. This may entail the complex questioning of people and the application of advanced statistical procedures to cull insight from the responses. After the research, your job is to draw a compelling story from the data that will provide guidance to a company—perhaps a Fortune 500 company—on whether and how to launch a new product or service. Heady work!

Market research also can be about "playing group therapist." Suppose you are conducting a focus group with 8 to 10 strangers. Your job is to cover an agenda of questions over the next 90 minutes. You need to motivate every member of the group to speak, reflect back to the group ideas that you are hearing, probe for the reasons people are saying what they are saying, and at no time bias what is being said. It can be a real mental workout.

But in moderating the group, your job is only half done. You then have to read through pages and pages of transcripts from the various group discussions. You will be looking for over-arching themes and specific commentary that illustrates these themes, because it will be this content that provides the basis for the story you now have to write—a story that answers your client's pressing business questions.

The other intellectually stimulating aspect of the work is the hours of conversations you will have with your colleagues coming up with an approach to a client's needs, or with your clients discussing research findings and the recommendations that follow from them. The atmosphere may be relaxed or charged. You may find others listening intently to what you have to say and nodding their agreement.

You may find yourself privy to a Fortune 500 company's plans. All the while you will be learning and growing as a person and as a professional market researcher.

It's that level of intellectual engagement in the work that has kept my rapt attention for over 40 years.

See the World

Market research offers the opportunity for lots of travel—some great, some not-so-great. I have had all-expenses-paid trips to Hong Kong, Singapore, Paris, London, Malta, Dubrovnik, Vienna, and the Caribbean. I also have gotten to go to places like Warsaw, Indiana—actually, a very likable small town.

In short, a career in market research is a sure-fire road to frequent business travel and lots of frequent flyer miles. While I have had my fair share of bumps along the way—delayed flights, late-night arrivals, and lousy meals in airports—they've been offset by some delightful travel experiences. Once I literally flew around the world first-class on my client's dime to observe and take note of face-to-face interviews with medical professionals on behalf of a major pharmaceutical company. There I was in Seoul, Korea sitting behind a one-way mirror hearing simultaneously-translated interviews. A few days later, I was doing the same thing, but this time in Paris.

Write the Future

At this point you may be asking yourself, "How long before I can expect to have these kinds of experiences?" Or you might be thinking, "Someone just entering into the field isn't going to get to meet with military generals and executive vice presidents of marketing."

That's true. In my generation, newcomers first had to spend five or more years in the trenches learning the mechanics of market research—presumably doing the boring stuff. But that apprenticeship scenario is changing and *must* change if the industry is going to attract the best and the brightest. Yes, you still need to learn the basics, which you will get primarily from on-the-job training, but that doesn't mean you will have no voice or visibility beyond your cubicle.

There's still another reason that market research is looking like an exciting career choice for up-and-comers—it's an industry that is expected to grow by 41 percent by 2020 (according to the U.S. Department of Labor). Much of this growth will be driven by the changes occurring in the industry. The field is undergoing an enormous shift, moving beyond the traditional structured surveys, embracing new data streams (e.g., Big Data, social media), and devising new ways to capture and report these data.

> Firms want to RECRUIT women and men well versed in social media and online consumption behaviors.

These shifts alone will open the doors widely for new blood. Firms want to recruit women and men well versed in social media and online consumption behaviors. Today's millennials know far more about the digital world than do their older counterparts. Don't be afraid to speak up and demonstrate your skills.

In the following chapters we will cover how to prepare for a career in market research, how to find that first job, how to move up the ladder, what you can expect to earn, and how market research can be a stepping-stone to other jobs.

CHAPTER 10

How Prepared Are You?

At this point you must be wondering what you have to know and do to get into this business. The industry is changing rapidly, particularly the role of market research suppliers. Success will require a combination of innate skills, acquired skills, and experience. These fundamentals are what I call "table stakes"—what you need to get your foot in the door.

> "I would tell anyone coming into market research to be good at the details, the fundamentals of this business, but not to obsess over the details. It's arguably more important to remain focused on the big picture—how the research findings fit into everything else that's going on in the organization. The most successful people will be the ones who can connect all the dots."
>
> —Ben Tolchinsky, Market Research Manager
> in a major communications company

> "I think the main thing that a company is looking for is very smart, analytically oriented, energetic young people who have a passion for wanting to learn market research. They have to be willing to work hard and learn the craft, be passionate about making

this a career, not just a job. Companies look for those who have not only the technical aptitude but also basic business smarts, someone who is well grounded and has good common sense."

—Rich Brenner, Market Research Industry Recruiter

Innate Skills

There are not a lot of skills you have to be born with to make it in market research, but there are a couple of essential ones. You're proba-

> Those likely to be interested in a market research career are most likely LEFT-BRAINED THINKERS: analytical, objective, and logical.

bly familiar with the concept of "left- and right-brained" people. Left-brained folks are purportedly analytical, objective, and logical, while right-brained thinkers are supposed to be more intuitive, thoughtful, and subjective. Despite the fact that science has disputed the reality of this cerebral dichotomy, it does serve to identify those likely to be interested in a market research as career—left-brained thinkers: analytical, objective, and logical.

Math skills are also important. While current cognitive research suggests that math skills can be learned, it is likely that we are all born with some math-related pre-wiring. At its core, the market research function is all about analyzing numbers and extracting meaning from them, so the market research professional needs to be well grounded in mathematics.

Certain personality traits will also serve you well:

- Empathy
- Patience
- Collaborative nature
- Flexibility/adaptability
- Self-confidence
- Self-motivation
- Curiosity

Learned Skills and Behaviors

The list of learned or acquired skills and behaviors is much longer and runs the gamut from the cognitive to the personal, social, and technical.

Cognitive skills are associated with one's ability to deal with data and include:

- the ability to see patterns in data sets
- the ability to integrate disparate data sets
- the ability to extract meaning from data
- the ability to display data in visual ways
- the aptitude of a good problem solver

Market research surveys generate answers to a set of well-constructed questions. In their raw form, these answers are tabulated by a computer and print out as a series of numbers in rows and columns. The rows are the answers and the columns are the ways in which the analyst wants to view the answers. In addition to the total sample, the results may be broken out by various demographic groups (e.g., men vs. woman, age groups, income groups) and cross-tabbed with answers to other questions (e.g., aware of brand vs. not aware of brand).

Does the table on page 116 make you feel dizzy, or are you ready to dive in and decode it? It is the market research analyst's job to look at the results of each question and find meaning in these numbers, link the data from multiple questions into some conclusions, and then visualize the results in ways that are compelling and easy to understand.

In the soft drink data in this table, do you see that the big take-away story is how consumption frequency varies by age? This story can be easily represented in the graph below the table, which boils down the data to its essentials and tells the story in a way that's clear at first glance.

Frequency of Soft Drink Consumption

		BANNER							
			AGE			GENDER			
Q9. Company A		Under 30	35 to 49	50 or more	NET	Male	Female	NET	TOTAL
Once every 3 months or less	% within column	21%↓	32%	38%	30%	23%↓	37%↑	30%	30%
	% within row	24%↓	32%	100%	100%	37%↓	63%↑	100%	100%
	Count	24	31	98	98	36	62	98	98
Once a month	% within column	12%	14%	14%	13%	16%	11%	13%	13%
	% within row	32%	32%	36%	100%	59%	41%	100%	100%
	Count	14	14	16	44	26	18	44	44
Once every 2 weeks	% within column	11%	7%	9%	9%	10%	8%	9%	9%
	% within row	43%	23%	33%	100%	53%	47%	100%	100%
	Count	13	7	10	30	16	14	30	30
LESS THAN WEEKLY	% within column	44%	53%	61%	53%	49%	56%	53%	54%
	% within row	30%	30%	40%	100%	45%	55%	100%	100%
	Count	51	52	69	172	78	94	172	172
Once a week	% within column	15%	20%	16%	17%	20%	14%	17%	37%
	% within row	31%	36%	33%	100%	58%	42%	100%	100%
	Count	17	20	18	55	32	23	55	55
2 to 5 days a week	% within column	25%	15%	18%	20%	23%	17%	20%	20%
	% within row	45%	23%	31%	100%	56%	44%	100%	100%
	Count	29	15	20	64	36	28	64	64
Every or nearly every day	% within column	16%	11%	5%	5%	11%	9%	13%	11%
	% within row	53%	31%	17%	17%	100%	39%	61%	100%
	Count	19	11	6	36	14	22	36	36
WEEKLY+	% within column	5%	47%	39%	47%	51%	44%	44%	47%
	% within row	42%	30%	28%	100%	53%	47%	47%	100%
	Count	65	46	44	155	82	82	73	155
TOTAL	% within column	100%	100%	100%	100%	100%	100%	100%	100%
	% within row	35%	30%	35%	100%	49%	51%	100%	100%
	Count	116	98	113	327	160	167	327	327
Average/year	Count	107.2 ↑	77.2	60.3 ↓	82.0	79.3	84.6	82.0	82.0

Frequency of Drinking Soft Drinks by Age

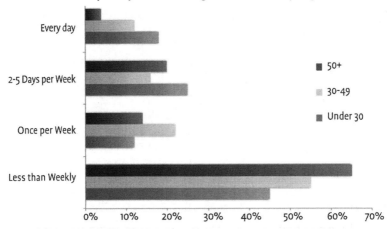

Other personal skills that can be developed on the job include:

- Skill in oral and written communications
- Excellent listening skills
- Reliability
- Leadership

The ability to speak well, write well, and command an audience is essential to any professional job, especially one in a service industry. If you are working for a research supplier your primary deliverables will be written documents in the form of proposals and reports. So it is paramount that you be a clear, concise writer. Not only must you have mastery of basic grammar and spelling, you must be able to extract a compelling story from hard data.

Market research studies are undertaken to answer one or more business questions—who is the market for our product, what features and functions should the product have, how should we position the product, and how are we doing. Prior to undertaking the research study you will spend a lot of time talking to your client about these questions. In order to do this well, you must be empathic; you must be able to put yourself in your client's shoes to understand his or her issues. Give your client room to talk. Be an active listener and ask clarifying questions as needed.

> It is the MARKET RESEARCH ANALYST'S JOB to look at the results of each question and find meaning in these numbers, link the learning from multiple questions into some conclusions, and then visualize the results in ways that are compelling and easy to understand.

When it comes time to present your proposal or present the findings of the research study in a group setting, the research analyst must hold the attention of the audience with both words and visuals and communicate with both presence and authority. Stan Sthanuathan, Global Vice President of Marketing Strategy and Insights at Coca-Cola, said it best in an article about research education:

"I am less worried about expertise in technical areas. Because if I hire people with strong technical skills—the kind of people that the research agencies hire—then we end up replicating the agencies' work internally and that is really unproductive. So what I look for is really solid storytelling skills, underpinned by best-in-class ability to connect the dots and deliver information with a lot of passion and enthusiasm."

Quirk's Marketing Research Review; June 2013
http://www.quirks.com/articles/2013/20130610.aspx

Whether you work on the client side or for a research supplier, you will be working in teams that require you to be collaborative, self-confident, and reliable. Market research companies, as well as corporate market research departments, vary in terms of the degree to which they are structured and follow exact protocols. In the absence of being given clear directions by those above you in the organization, you will never go wrong by demonstrating self-motivation and initiative. These are behaviors that are valued in the market research industry.

> Successful market research agencies and corporate departments don't just deliver reports. They must act as CHANGE AGENTS for their clients and in their companies.

Having the core technical skills to do market research is just the price of entry. Those who will rise in the ranks also must have consultative and leadership skills. Successful market research agencies and corporate departments don't just deliver reports. They must act as change agents for their clients and in their companies. They have to foster engagement and gain the trust of senior managers to help ensure that the research findings get translated into a set of goals and action steps.

Finally, a career in market research requires that you be adaptable, flexible, and forward thinking. As mentioned throughout these pages, the field of market research is constantly changing and you must keep pace.

Technical knowledge. In addition to what you will bring to market research in the form of your innate and learned personal skills, there are technical skills that you will need to acquire either through your academic training or on the job. These include:

- **Research skills**—survey design, modes of data collection, questionnaire construction, sampling, statistics, advanced analytics, and programming
- **Organizational skills**—project management
- **Business know-how**—basic marketing, knowledge of different industries, knowledge of how businesses make decisions

Much of this core knowledge can be learned in college if you major in fields like psychology and business or pursue a degree or certificate specifically in market research. But what if you've arrived at this point with a degree in English or anthropology? Most people who've majored in other subjects but aspire to a career in market research find it's entirely possible to learn many of these skills on the job.

Sources of Training

If you are about to enter college or are currently in college and are considering market research as a career, be sure your undergraduate course of study includes at least some, if not all, of these foundational courses:

- Introductory Psychology
- Introductory Sociology
- Basic Statistics
- Introductory Marketing
- Introductory Economics

In addition to these, consider taking three more courses in the Psychology department:

- **Social Psychology**—about attitudes, perceptions, and group behavior; ideal in that market research is actually applied Social Psychology.
- **Cognitive Processes**—where you will learn about human decision-making.

- **Consumer Psycholog**y—probably as close as you will come to an academic introduction to the world of market research.

The following are some basic questions that you may be asking:

Question 1: Do I need a graduate degree?

A master's degree is not imperative, but it won't hurt, and in a tight job market it may give you a competitive advantage. For starters, going for your master's degree will give you a chance to accumulate more knowledge and skills than you can pick up as an undergraduate. You might be able to gain some on-the-job experience in a market research internship. In my own case, my summer jobs during graduate school gave me an invaluable first exposure to the field.

After I finished my undergraduate degree, I immediately entered a master's degree program in psychology and finished in two years. My first job upon completing that program, and prior to my starting my PhD work, was in the market research department of an advertising agency in Chicago. The fellow who hired me made the following Catch-22ish comment to me upon my arrival: "I wouldn't have hired you without your MA, but I would have preferred that you had been working for these past two years."

Question 2: So what degree should I pursue?

A master's degree in any of the social sciences (e.g., psychology, sociology, political science) is great in terms of the concepts and research techniques you will learn. A business MBA in marketing also is ideal. Here you will have the opportunity to learn both the fundamentals of general business and those specific to marketing. Most MBA programs also offer one or two basic courses in market research.

An increasing number of business schools are offering a master's degree in market research. The following is a list of some of the best programs in the United States.

University of Georgia	The Coca-Cola Center for Marketing Studies	Athens, GA
	Terry College of Business	
University of Wisconsin	A.C. Nielsen Center for Marketing Research	Madison, WI
University of Texas at Arlington	McCombs School of Business	Arlington, TX
Michigan State University	Broad Graduate School of Management	East Lansing, MI
DePaul University	Kellstadt Graduate School of Business	Chicago, IL
Clemson University	College of Business and Behavioral Science	Clemson, SC
Southern Illinois University	School of Business	Edwardsville, IL
Rutgers University	Rutgers Business School	Piscataway, NJ

There also are academic programs in Survey Research Methodology offered in departments other than the business school, such as that offered by the Institute for Social Research at the University of Michigan in Ann Arbor or Northwestern University's Medill School of Journalism in Evanston, IL, which offers an MS in Integrated Marketing Communications. The latter program includes courses in market research, statistics, market segmentation, and customer loyalty. Another program is the MS in Survey Research and Methodology offered by the University of Nebraska in Lincoln.

There are numerous online and certificate programs in market research which may consist of a small number of core courses that are offered either for credit or no credit. These are ideal for someone post-college who may be looking to make a career change or for those already working in market research who feel they need additional training. Here is a list of some of the better known certificate programs.

Fairleigh Dickinson University	Petrocelli College of Continuing Studies	Teaneck, NJ
Northwestern University	School of Continuing Studies	Evanston, IL
University of Georgia	Center for Continuing Education	Athens, GA
University of Illinois/Chicago	Department of Public Administration	Chicago, IL
University of Maryland	Joint Program in Survey Methodology	College Park, MD
The George Washington University	Graduate Education Center	Alexandria, VA

Finally, I am familiar with at least one undergraduate program in market research. The Illinois Institute of Technology in Chicago has recently introduced a Bachelor of Science in Consumer Research, Analytics, and Communication in its Lewis College of Human Sciences.

Who Will Be Hired?

At the beginning of this chapter I noted there are many fundamental skills and personal traits that you need for success and longevity in market research. The field is no longer dominated by surveys and focus groups. Big Data and social media have created a virtual "fire hose" of information about what people are doing and saying that must be taken into consideration. To an increasing degree the focus for marketers will be on integrating these different data streams. There always will be a need to know how to do market research, so there will always be a role for the traditional market research supplier, the skilled technician. However, the integration of disparate data coupled with the increasing automation of the market research process means that the role of the market researcher will be more about providing insight and strategy rather than just technical expertise.

> The role of the market researcher will be more about providing INSIGHT AND STRATEGY rather than technical expertise.

I asked several market research veterans what they see as the future for market research suppliers and market researchers.

"Market researchers of tomorrow will need to possess different skills than those of today. An expertise in survey research, long the staple of the industry, will no longer suffice. They will need to learn to work effectively with new and different information—social media posts, online and offline footprints, images and video, and transaction databases to name a few—or they may find themselves out of a job, if they've got one at all. But if they take a different path and learn to make sense of the many data sources to which they have access and, in turn, offer great advice, they'll become indispensable. I, for one, know which path I would take."
—George Terhanian, Chief Research and Analytics Officer
NPD Group

"The future of market research lies in becoming more of a science than an art, particularly with the introduction of new methodologies which incorporate things like neurological testing. Our data will come under much more public and private scrutiny, meaning that we as an industry must become even more diligent about the way things are done to ensure the data can withstand scrutiny. Going forward, there will be an increasing emphasis on insights driven by Big Data and heavy analytics. I fear our current lines of training in the industry don't include much in the way of Big Data and heavy analytics. Schools will need to find ways to access data and incorporate new training to ensure the next generation of researchers isn't forced to learn that skill on the job."
—Dan Kirkland, North American Consumer Insights Leader,
Nielsen

"The atmosphere of the industry is changing, evidenced by the debate over whether market researchers of the future are destined to have their value questioned, particularly when it comes to the client-side audience. More and more research specialists are inundated with wave after wave of technology solutions including social media research, quick polls, do-it-yourself tools, ready-made web-based survey audiences—all in the face of company-enforced budget reductions. These advances in technology may signal a change in market research as it has been known, but they will also enable the researcher to be creative in exploring many more parameters of any given business problem. Ultimately the field still requires someone at the helm to steer and interpret the results that all the new technology provides."

—Paul Burnett, former Market Research Director, McGladrey

"I see a couple of trends continuing and accelerating:

- Industry specialization—where market research suppliers are expected to come to the table with deep knowledge of the client's competitive environment and to add value as a consulting partner.

- An increasing role for suppliers in integrating multiple information sources to create a more comprehensive picture—primary, secondary, internal client data, web analytics, social listening, mobile, real-time VOC [Voice of the Customer], etc.

"The challenge for marketing research organizations going forward is to develop industry and data integration competencies in addition to maintaining strong expertise with traditional methods."

—Roger Brown, Director – Market Research,
Northwestern Mutual

"We are going through a period of disruptive change. Some market research companies will take advantage of that change and thrive. Other will fail to grasp the opportunities and will die. The expertise of our discipline is the aggregation of multi-source information and making sense of it. Historically, this has been done casually. The sources and tools are now different, but the innate curiosity of a researcher and his or her ability to weave a story together from disparate data sources will remain the core value of what we produce. Personally, I think we are entering into yet another golden age for market research. The next decade is going to be a thrill."

—Jeff Resnick, Managing Partner,
Stakeholder Advisory Services, LLC

Cambiar LLC, a consulting firm that advises research agencies and corporate insight departments, conducted a study on the future of market research* that is a must-read for anyone in market research or considering a career in the field. The report is readily available on the internet. Cambiar interviewed both corporate and agency researchers and asked them how they see the industry changing in the next decade through 2020. A few of their key findings are particularly noteworthy.

First, virtually everyone interviewed agreed that successful market researchers will have great consulting skills. Second, the role of corporate researchers will require them "to lead, educate, and inspire their internal customers." Agency researchers will "need to focus on business outcomes rather than research outputs, to gain skills in order to facilitate being strategic partners, and to strengthen their understanding of the client's business."

The report concluded with the following key takeaways for suppliers and corporate researchers alike:

"Full-service research companies must become 'Integrated Research Agencies.' These agencies will have a culture of working collaboratively, both internally and with clients; the skills to

---

* *The Future of Research Report*, October 2011. (http://www.consultcambiar.com/wp-content/uploads/2010/06/CambiarFutureofResearchReport_2011.pdf).

synthesize information from numerous sources; and the ability to create presentations that tell stories from the research; and they will get the client's business so that they become a true partner in getting to the 'Now What?'

"Corporate research departments must partner with research companies that have these capabilities. A new way of working is needed, along with a re-evaluation of research company partners; and a new business model that is consistent with hiring an agency versus hiring a supplier or vendor."

Clearly the future for market research entails an elevated role, one that means that the successful practitioners will be those who have sharpened skills and can make the most of their professional talents.

CHAPTER 11

Getting Hired

In the introduction I noted that most people in market research will admit having "stumbled" into the career. While that may lead to a positive outcome for some, I hope your pursuit of your first market research job will be more structured and better informed. Landing a job in this field is no different than pursuing a job in many other professional service industries. Keep an open mind and be flexible, because there is no one "right" course to pursue. You may need to combine several approaches, particularly if you're just graduating from college.

Good News and Bad News

The good news is that the market research industry is growing. Many corporations are expanding their consumer insights departments and research suppliers are also hiring. The bad news is that there are a great many qualified entry-level people in the job market. Having relevant academic training is merely the first hurdle; experience will always separate the more attractive from the less attractive candidates.

The best geographical markets to find a job in market research are the major cities (e.g., Boston, New York, Philadelphia, Atlanta, Chicago, Dallas, Houston, Los Angeles, San Francisco, and Seattle) where the majority of market research firms and many major corporations are based. The good news is that many market research suppliers allow their well-established employees to work remotely from home. This is never a good option for the entry-level employee who will want to work where he/she can get training and ongoing exposure to senior staff.

Finding a job in market research can present a classic Catch-22 situation. How do you get experience if no one will hire you without it? There are ways around this obstacle. For starters, apply for Interviewing jobs and internships in your college community or over the summer. Despite the clustering of opportunities in major cities, the market research industry operates throughout the country. Nielsen, the world's largest information services company, with offices in more than two dozen U.S. cities, runs a formal internship program for college students and hires a number of its interns upon graduation. If you are still an undergraduate or graduate student, investigate relevant internships in your university's psychology or sociology departments. Also consider conducting a few surveys of your own design, using do-it-yourself survey tools like Survey Monkey and Zoomerang. These online tools are easy to use and make it possible for virtually anyone to try their hand at market research. You can use your friends and family as respondents. It will give you experience in designing, running, analyzing, and reporting a small survey. Moreover, it will enable you to tell a prospective employer, "Yes, I have conducted surveys in the past."

In addition to picking up experience wherever you can, keep educating yourself about the field. Take advantage of the various industry resources, publications, and social media to stay up to date on job openings, job-seeking advice, and industry trends. Look for industry conferences to attend. All of the conferences have special discounted fees for students.

Become familiar with leading industry organizations including the Council of American Survey Research Organizations (CASRO, casro.org), the American Marketing Association (AMA, ama.org) and the Marketing Research Association (MRA, marketingresearchassociation.org). Each group provides ample information and resources for anyone looking to enter the industry or make a job change.

LinkedIn (www.linkedin.com) is a boon to anyone looking to learn who's who in the industry and network with professionals already in the field. In addition, LinkedIn has numerous subgroups organized around various aspects of market research. The best one for those coming into the industry is the Marketing Research & Insights Group. Market Research Professionals is another good group to consider.

Speaking of industry trends, the increased focus on Big Data and social media requires people with strong skills in all things digital: data mining, infographics, math, and statistical software packages like SPSS and SAS. Make every effort to pick up some, if not all, of these skills while still in school or immediately after.

Get a subscription to *Quirk's Marketing Research Review,* a well-recognized monthly publication providing topical articles about general issues and trends, case studies, industry news, conference information, background on research suppliers, and a calendar of industry events. Loaded with names of individuals, titles, and companies, it's a great resource for the job seeker. *Quirk*'s June 2013 issue, referenced earlier, presented a valuable article ("Next in Line, Please," page 58) on what companies are looking for in their new market research hires and what students in market research education programs were being taught. The publication interviewed a

> Get a subscription to QUIRK'S MARKETING RESEARCH REVIEW for topical articles about general issues and trends, case studies, industry news, conference information, background on research suppliers, and a calendar of industry events. Loaded with names of individuals, titles, and companies, it's a great resource for the job seeker.

number of employers and educators for the article. Here are a few noteworthy takeaways:

> "We teach market research methodologies that are used to find consumer insights. But our program has a strong focus on what to do with those insights: synthesize and integrate them with the whole business and drive impact on the marketing and business strategy."
>
> —Kristin Branch
> Director of the A.C. Nielsen Center for Marketing Research
> University of Wisconsin

> "We aim to have a highly rigorous program with a heavy dose of skills—especially quantitative—combined with business acumen and consultative skills. My advisory board emphasizes the need for technically skilled graduates who truly understand the business questions and applications and who can communicate with different stakeholders."
>
> —Charlotte Mason, Director
> Coca-Cola Center for Marketing Studies, University of Georgia

> "On a more macro level, we believe that more emphasis on leadership skills and understanding business dynamics would be beneficial. Additionally, programs that, at a minimum, touch upon skill sets like data visualization and data integration would improve traditional market research curricula."
>
> —Holly Jarrell, Chief Client Services Officer
> GfK Consumer Experiences North America

And finally, one of the best quotes in terms of what employees are looking for:

> "My wish list for new employees includes a passion for knowledge, adaptability, fearless creativity, confidence in front of a group, and the ability to tell a convincing story. Regardless of their research specialty, be it digital media, quantitative research, social listening or anything else, it is vital they understand the entire research landscape. It is not necessary to be a master of every

technique; they just need to have a holistic awareness of the tools that are available to address every challenge."

—Kym Frank, Vice President, Strategic Insights, Optimedia

Female Friendly

The market research industry always has been friendly to women. The majority of jobs are held by women, including many of the senior managerial and executive positions. A 2014 study by the employee search firm CareerCast identified "market research analyst" as one of the top 12 jobs for women in the U.S. in 2014. The firm examined some 200 careers and made its selections based on the number of women working in the field, average annual salaries, gender equality in pay, projected hiring, and lifestyle factors like physical demands and stress. According to their study, the average annual salary for females in market analyst positions was $60,000. They also cited Bureau of Labor Statistics projections that the number of women in this career track would increase by 32 percent by 2022.

What You Will Do

The typical entry-level position in marketing research, whether on the client side or with a supplier, will have various job titles such as Research Assistant, Research Associate, or Analyst. If you are hired by a research agency, you likely will find yourself spending your first months performing support tasks such as checking data tabulations, posting tables (i.e., creating PowerPoint graphs of the findings), or proofreading

> BE PROACTIVE. Keep your eyes open for learning opportunities, ask questions, volunteer for extra assignments.

reports. You will likely receive some formal training on all aspects of the firm's particular approach to the market research process. As you progress, you will be given more challenging responsibilities including writing reports, preparing a project budget, and coordinating interviewing and data processing.

If your first position is on the client side, you may find yourself co-ordinating the work of your research agency partners and preparing summary reports.

Be proactive. Keep your eyes open for learning opportunities, ask questions, volunteer for extra assignments, etc. Step outside your comfort zone to move your career along.

The Value of a Mentor

Irrespective of which side of the research fence you work, you likely will be working in a team comprised of more senior colleagues, one or more of whom will supervise your work. If you are really lucky, one of those early supervisors might turn out to be a mentor of sorts, someone who will teach you technical and client-related skills. I encourage you to seek out a real mentor, someone who is not just a teacher but also a go-to source for advice and encouragement.

Most successful people have had someone in whom they could confide and who offered them guidance throughout their career. By definition, a mentor is going to be someone who has years of experience in your field and the concomitant wisdom that accrues from that experience. Accordingly, he or she provides you with a learned perspective that you, as a newcomer, will not have. Your mentor also will look out for you, identify opportunities and possible pitfalls, and help you successfully navigate your career path. Your mentor should **not** be your direct supervisor, but should be someone with whom you can comfortably share your insecurities, concerns, and ambitions.

The Resume

Okay, suppose you're a recent graduate ready to put yourself out there and find that entry-level job. The first step is to create a resume that will catch someone's attention. If you are just coming out of school, you may be short on hands-on experience, but you can put your best spin on your educational qualifications and the relevant skills you will bring to the job. The hiring manager will be trying to discern what kind of person you are. Let your personality come through. Demonstrate that you are a serious, enthusiastic, and engaging person. Communicate clearly.

The goal of submitting a resume is twofold—get it read by a prospective employer and be invited to an interview. Your resume is likely to be one of thousands received. In many cases, your resume may not be read initially by a human. Rather, it will be scanned by a computer on the lookout for key information and wording. You want your resume to break through this clutter and motivate someone to want to meet you.

There are many books and websites that can instruct you on how to write an effective resume. Any of these will provide you with advice on the two key elements of any resume: **content** and **format.** I encourage you to study these resources for best-in-class examples. Summarizing the resources, the following are some of the most important elements of writing a successful resume:

Content	Format
Contact information: (name, address, email, phone)	Limit to 2 pages
Customize to the job you are applying for	Provide a short compelling summary of your goals and what you will bring to the employer
Career goals	Use clean fonts (e.g., Arial)
Employment history	Use bullets and short sentences and lots of spacing
Skills relevant to the job you are seeking	
	Avoid use of personal pronouns
Emphasize achievements	Quantify achievements (e.g., supervised 10 professionals)
Education	
Awards & honors	
References (only upon request)	

Finally, be sure to proofread your resume carefully. The fastest way to get your resume tossed into the trash is to have spelling and grammatical errors. So ask a trusted advisor to read your resume and give you critical feedback before sending it.

The Interview

Do your research! Be prepared! In no particular order, here are a few essential rules when interviewing.

- ✓ **Rule 1 – Know your company.** Come to every interview with an in-depth knowledge of the company. If you are interviewing for a client-side position, also know their position within the industry and current industry issues and challenges. If you are interviewing with a market research supplier, find out what differentiates that firm from its competitors. Here the Internet is your best friend. Do Google searches on the company and its competitors, and study its website. Try to get a handle on the corporate culture, and read what is being said about the company in social media.

- ✓ **Rule 2 – Show your knowledge of market research.** Be conversant about techniques and trends. You should be able to demonstrate that you have a sound grasp of the fundamentals of market research—how it is used and how it is done. Show that you are familiar with the latest technologies (e.g., mobile data collection) and new directions (e.g., Big Data).

- ✓ **Rule 3 – Think on your feet.** Your interviewer may pose an out-of-the-box question to see *how* you think and whether you can handle a little stress. You can count on this happening if you are applying for a position other than entry-level. For starters, do a Google search to find out the kinds of questions interviewers like to ask, and role play with a friend. A typical question might be "Describe a particularly stressful situation you faced and how you handled it."

✓ **Rule 4 – Show your interest.** Come to the interview with a list of questions related to this particular company and the market research role. A certain level of curiosity is appealing and helps you make a genuine connection with your interviewer, but be careful not to come across as a know it all.

✓ **Rule 5 – Why you?** Be prepared to answer the question "Why should we hire you?" or "What will you bring to this job?" Be honest, realistic, and specific. Focus on the personal character traits that make you a strong potential hire.

✓ **Rule 6 – Be enthusiastic and engaging.** Master the basics: maintain eye contact and offer a strong handshake.

I highly recommend that you read *Good in a Room: How to Sell Yourself (and Your Ideas) and Win Over Any Audience* by Stephanie Palmer.* It is an excellent resource for how to be prepared, highly effective, poised, and confident in an interview and, indeed, in any business meeting. All in all, Palmer teaches a set of interpersonal skills that will come in handy throughout your career.

Salary and Benefits

In market research compensation is based on a salary and bonus. At senior levels, there may be additional compensation in the form of company stock as well as perks like a company car. Market research senior executives typically earn six-figure incomes—$150,000 to $250,000. On the supplier side, those who are in a sales role have the opportunity to make six-figure incomes long before they reach senior executive status. These individuals are likely to receive a salary plus sales commissions. If they are very successful, their commissions may exceed their base salary.

---

* *Good in a Room: How to Sell Yourself (and Your Ideas) and Win Over Any Audience,* Stephanie Palmer, Doubleday, © 2008.

In its 2014 annual salary and compensation survey of its subscribers, Quirk's surveyed over 3,000 individuals in both corporate and supplier market research jobs. On average, supplier-side researchers were earning slightly more than their corporate-side counterparts.

Supplier = $129K   **Corporate** = $123K

Average salaries by job level were as follows:

SUPPLIER		CORPORATE	
Title	Average Salary (thousands)	Title	Average Salary (thousands)
SVP/VP	$189	Market Research Director	$174
Sr. Project Director	$91	Market Research Manager	$119
Project Director	$67	Project Manager	$104
Research Associate	$49	Sr. Research Analyst	$87
Statistician	$107	Research Analyst	$68
Business Development	$82	Research Assistant	$58

For entry-level researchers, the pay is going to be much lower. According to the same 2014 Quirk's industry study, the average **starting salary** was in the mid-to-high forties, with those working on the client side earning a bit more than those hired by market research firms

Supplier = $45K   **Corporate** = $48K

In addition to salary, you will be provided with health and disability insurance benefits. As you move up the ladder, there will be opportunities to earn cash bonuses based on your group's and/or company's performance. You also may receive a credit card for your work-related travel expenses and a company-provided mobile device.

CHAPTER 12

Career Progression:
Climbing the Ladder and Criteria for Success

Whether you find yourself in a market research agency or in a client organization, there will be essentially three job levels—entry/junior, mid/experienced, and senior. Any good-size market research agency is likely to staff numerous job functions and levels within each job category—research assistant, research associate, senior research associate; project manager, project director, research manager; consultant, senior consultant, etc. As you progress into senior positions, officer titles like Vice President (VP), Senior Vice President (SVP), and Executive Vice President (EVP) get overlaid onto the job role—such as SVP, Senior Consultant.

Sellers and Doers

For those on the research agency side of the industry, there is another differentiator that will define your career path: are you a *Seller* or *Doer?*

Regarding the *Seller* role, there are pure sales roles and research-based sales roles. More about *Sellers* later in this chapter.

Doers, by definition, do the research work, and the vast majority of those who begin a career in market research are hired in this role.

Most people want to be involved in the design, execution, and reporting of research. However, there are important support functions like sampling, survey programming, data processing, data collection, and advanced analytics that are critical to any market research firm. All large agencies staff these functions in-house, although some firms outsource telephone interviewing.

Many market research professionals have long and lucrative careers within each of these areas, never moving outside their specialty. People with strong programming skills may gravitate to programming or data processing departments. Others with especially strong statistical skills may find their home in an advanced analysis group, now usually called a Marketing Science department. Each of these specialties can offer satisfying career opportunities as well as lucrative pay as you progress up the ranks.

The Doer Journey

Let's take a look at what the journey is for *Research Doers*—what you may find yourself doing as you move from a junior to a mid-level to a senior role.

Junior Researcher

The operative term for beginning a new job is **onboarding.** The term refers to an orientation period—consisting of a couple of days to a couple of weeks—during which you are set up with the basic tools you will need to do your job, like a computer and email, as well as learn about the company's policies, procedures, and benefits. You'll spend a lot of time completing forms, reading documents, and looking at online presentations. However, what you won't get, unless you are in a very large agency, is much formal training. Historically, training in the market research industry has been *baptism by fire,* meaning you are expected to learn on the job.

If you are in a research agency, you likely will be assigned to a small team that is working with specific clients or on a specific type of research. This research category may be defined either by industry (e.g., retail, financial services, pharma, etc.) or by marketing issue (e.g., customer loyalty, brand strategy, advertising testing, etc.).

As an entry-level researcher in an agency your responsibilities will be largely related to survey operational tasks. Here is a list of the typical tasks you will be asked to do:

Junior-Level Research Tasks

- Test survey questionnaires
- Monitor data collection
- Write data tabulation instructions
- Proofread data tabulations
- Post survey results in graphical format
- Proofread reports

What client interaction you have will be largely just sitting in, but not talking, during phone conferences and in-person meetings.

Within a short period of time you will be given the opportunity to write commentary on top of survey findings presented in reports. See an example below.

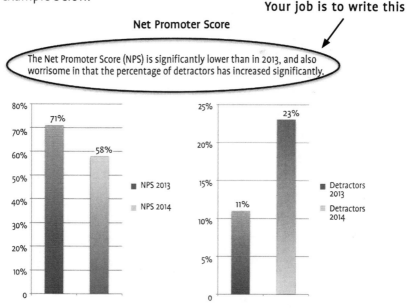

Your job is to write this

Net Promoter Score

The Net Promoter Score (NPS) is significantly lower than in 2013, and also worrisome in that the percentage of detractors has increased significantly.

entry-level junior researcher will likely involve managing suppliers and helping those above you prepare summary reports and presentations to management based on the surveys you have commissioned.

> Historically, TRAINING in the market research industry has been baptism by fire, meaning you are expected to learn on the job.

Your success, and the likelihood and timing of your promotions, will be judged on the basis of how quickly you master the responsibilities you are given, how well you demonstrate your increasing knowledge of research operations and methodologies, and your personal skills. In particular, a junior staffer is evaluated on the basis of:

- Oral and written communications
- Ability to listen well
- Ability to collaborate
- Self-confidence
- Reliability
- Self-motivation
- Adaptability

Mid-Level Researcher

Within a couple of years you should expect to move into roles where you are given more responsibility. On the agency side this will include writing questionnaires, running budgets for proposals, interacting with clients, more report writing, and the supervision of junior staff. Given your interests and depending on how your company is structured, you also may conduct in-depth interviews on qualitative projects.

At the more senior-end of this tier, you will be expected to participate in internal company planning activities focusing on a wide variety of issues such as account planning, sales initiatives, staff welfare, training, and the like. You also may find yourself managing more people.

On the client side, the mid-level staffer will play more of an ombudsman role between internal clients and research suppliers. You will meet with your internal clients to listen to their needs, then translate those needs into a request for a proposal (RFP), assess and choose suppliers for your projects, manage suppliers, and present the results back to your internal clients.

Once again, your success will be determined by how well you master your increased responsibilities and demonstrate your growing knowledge of all aspects of market research. You will continue to be evaluated on the same personal skills. In addition, your management skills will become a significant factor in your evaluation.

Senior-Level Researcher

It likely will take you at least 10 years to reach this level in a major market research firm. At this point in your career there will be several different paths that you can take. Many of the research professionals I have known and worked with over the years have been quite happy carving out a career as a *Doer* and love the process of designing, executing, and reporting a research project. These folks have no interest in selling and may even fear the sales role.

The Sales Role

Selling, whether it is market research or any other service or product, involves some calculation of trade-offs. On one hand, there is an opportunity to make a lot of money. Some of the highest paid individuals in market research are dedicated sales specialists who earn both a salary and commissions. On the other hand, selling requires a combination of strong personal skills that you may or may not have.

The sales role in a market research firm also involves substantial risk. Salespeople have sales targets they must meet. A typical target may be $500,000 in the first year, quickly doubling to $1 million and

higher in the next year. When they don't achieve these targets, senior management may ques-
tion their value to the firm. **Great communicator**
The highest turnover I have
witnessed in research agen- **Engaging personality**
cies over the years has been
among the sales force. **Ability to think fast on your feet**

    The fact that many mar-
ket research professionals **A thick skin to deal with rejection**
shy away from sales is not all that surprising. People with strong
analytical minds—the kind of people who gravitate towards market
research—are often more introverted than others. It's the old left-
brain right-brain dichotomy.

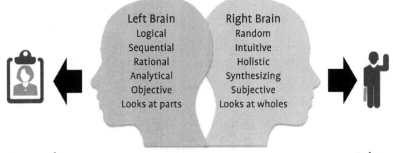

Researcher   **Sales**

The Consultant Role: Business Developer and Researcher

From my perspective, one of the best senior-level roles has a dual
focus: both business development and research. In many large firms
this staff position is called a **consultant**. In small boutique agencies,
this role is undertaken by the firm's principals. It's the role I played
for much of my career. It gave me the opportunity to keep my hands
in the research, but also enjoy the excitement and intellectual challenge of listening to clients' needs, write and present proposals to
address those needs, and then win the engagement.

    Unlike the dedicated market research sales person, I rarely had to do any "cold calling" into companies to find opportunities. More often, I was the guy who was brought in *after* the opportunity had been identified by others whose job was to do the cold calling. My role was to listen to the client's needs and talk about how we might address them. I took the lead on writing and presenting our proposals. When we won the work, I provided thought leadership on the questionnaire and then on the interpretation of the findings. At this juncture in my career, I rarely got too involved in the day-to-day survey operations.

If you aspire to the consultant role, you will likely act as a specialist in one or several areas. For many years, I specialized in all aspects of research focusing on the customer experience. This included work on measuring satisfaction following a transaction, or the relational loyalty of customers to a company or brand, or why they were defecting. Other of my colleagues who were also consultants specialized in issues like brand strategy, corporate reputation, or advertising research. In some firms consultants are differentiated on the basis of their industry expertise—for example, financial, industrial, pharma, hospitality, and the like.

> Your ability to ENGAGE AND COMMAND ATTENTION AND RESPECT from your clients or internal stakeholders will be critical to your success.

Other Senior-Level Roles

Other senior-level professionals find great satisfaction in managing a group of researchers. In this role your focus will be on survey operations, overseeing P&L statements for your group, and managing people. You will continue to have client responsibilities and be involved in individual projects.

On the client side, the senior role may find you heading your company's research function or leading a particular area of research (e.g., new products, customer acquisition, customer experience, marketing communications, brand strategy, and so on).

At this stage of your career, success will continue to be measured by all of the previous criteria plus new ones. If you are involved in business development, considerable weight will be attached to the amount of business you generate. You will be given targets to meet that are aggressive and increase year over year. Your leadership skills also will be at the forefront of your evaluations, irrespective of what role you fill. Whether you are on the agency side or client side, your ability to engage and command attention and respect from your clients or internal stakeholders will be critical to your success.

Some Fast-Track Options

Thus far I have described a rather basic roadmap to entering and progressing through a career in market research. This route will characterize the career journey for the great majority of those who enter the field. However, as in any profession, there are exceptions to the rule, ways in which you can jump-start or fast-track your career. Let's look at a couple of these options.

The Power of a PhD

Having a doctorate degree is not a requirement for a successful career in market research. Nevertheless, there are many companies that like to shout about the number of PhD's they have on staff. I speak from experience here, because this is how I accelerated my career.

Achieving PhD-level training in any relevant field like psychology, sociology, political science, economics, or marketing means that you have deep subject-matter knowledge, solid research skills, and excellent oral and written communication skills. In a tight job market, this skill set will make you stand out from the crowd and put you ahead of many of your competitors.

I put in my time as a junior researcher off and on while I was in graduate school. Upon completing my PhD in psychology, I came to the attention of a small boutique firm in Chicago looking to "hire a PhD or two" for no other reason than having a staff with this academic credential helped differentiate their firm in the marketplace. The preference for hiring PhD's was, in part, the result of the fact that one of the firm's two principals was a well-known university marketing professor whom everyone had to call "Doctor." Even his partner called him Doctor.

I stayed at this firm for three years when again the call for a PhD came from one of the largest firms in the industry at the time. As mentioned earlier, this organization had a major contract with the U.S. Department of Defense to conduct marketing surveys to help guide recruitment strategy and tactics for the all-volunteer military. A number of the clients were PhD's, and the firm felt it needed a PhD to go "man-to-man" with the client. I became their man and my career quickly skipped over some of the middle years. I was elevated to the role of a VP-Consultant at age 31.

Digital Prowess

The new frontiers of marketing are being defined by all things digital—mobile apps to manage our lives, digital marketing, and social media to name a few. This fact has tremendous implications for the market research industry. Forward-thinking companies are looking to add staff with expertise in Big Data and digital media. Having either or both digital technical skills and an understanding of how to view and interpret consumers' digital behavior will differentiate the job applicant and be a career propellant.

> Within market research, the key digital skills will be ANALYTICAL AND STRATEGIC. Increasingly, market researchers will be asked to interpret and offer guidance on what new data streams mean.

The need for people with digital technical skills is underscored by a 2012 report by the consulting firm Capgemini (pronounced *cap Gemini*) that stated that over 4.4 million IT jobs will be created around Big Data by 2015. While those going into market research may not need to have the specialized engineering skills to create and manage digital media, they will be well served by a technical understanding.* The same report referenced a 2009 study conducted by the research firm IDC which noted: "By 2015, 90 percent of all jobs will require Information and communication technology (ICT) skills. Business professionals will increasingly need to be comfortable with digital tools and technologies in order to perform their core roles."

Within market research, the key digital skills will be analytical and strategic. Increasingly, market researchers will be asked to interpret and offer guidance on what these new data streams mean. Those able to do this will fast-track to the forefront of their departments or agencies.

---

* Capgemini Consulting – MIT Center for Digital Business Research, *The Digital Advantage: How digital leaders outperform their peers in every industry*, 2012.

APPENDIX I

Career Information Resources

"I say, follow your bliss and don't be afraid, and doors will open where you didn't know they were going to be."

—Joseph Campbell

Having read this book, you now have a better handle on what market research is, the scope of the industry, and its prospects for growth. You also know what a career in this field requires from you and what you can expect to do on the job. I've tried to cover all of the major issues and anticipate most of your questions. My goal has been to fill what I know to be the information gap for those considering a market research career. No single source, however, can provide everything that one would want or need to know about the industry. What follows is a list of some of the best additional resources to consult to learn more about the past, present, and future of market research.

I wish you great success in choosing your career and on the journey that you will take.

—JTH

Associations

Key market research industry associations:

American Association for Public Opinion Research	www.aapor.org
American Marketing Association	www.ama.org
Advertising Research Foundation	www.thearf.org
American Statistical Association	www.amstat.org
Association for Consumer Research	www.acrwebsite.org
Council of American Survey Research Organizations (CASRO)	www.casro.org
European Society for Opinion and Marketing Research (ESOMAR)	www.esomar.org
Interactive Market Research Association	www.imro.org
Marketing Research Association	www.marketingresearch.org
Qualitative Research Consultants Association	www.qrca.org
The Market Research Society (MRS)	www.mrs.org.uk

Publications/Websites

Publications and websites you should be familiar with:

Quirk's Marketing Research Review

Marketing News (American Marketing Association)

Research-Live.com

Journal of Consumer Research

Journal of Marketing Research

Paramount Market Publishing, Inc.

RFL Communications, Inc.

GreenBook—A Guide for Buyers of Marketing Research

LinkedIn Groups

LinkedIn is an excellent resource for keeping abreast of the current dialogues going on in the industry, as well as identifying people working in the field.

Market Research

Marketing Research Association

Next Gen Market Research

The Market Research Event

The Marketing Research Insights Group

International Market Research Society

Market Research in the Mobile World

Future Trends

Consumer Insights Interest Group

Market Research Data Visualization

Innovation and New Tools in Market Research

Competitive/Market Intelligence Professionals

Infographics & Data Visualization

Advanced Business Analytics,
    Data Mining and Predictive Modeling

Market Research Professionals

Consumer Psychology

Some Must-Read Market Research Books

These books will enhance your knowledge of the field. Those shown in **bold italic** are the recommendations of a 2013 survey by Quirk's of its Marketing Research & Insights LinkedIn group in which they asked members "What books should a marketing researcher be required to read?"

Aldridge, Alan and Kenneth Levine. ***Surveying the Social World: Principles and Practice in Survey Research.*** Buckingham and

Philadelphia: Open University Press, 2001.

Atkinson, Cliff. *Beyond Bullet Points: Using Microsoft PowerPoint to Create Presentations that Inform, Motivate, and Inspire.* Redmond: Microsoft Press, 2005.

Barabba, Vincent and Gerald Zaltman. *Hearing the Voice of the Market: Competitive Advantage Through Creative Use of Market Information.* Boston: Harvard Business School Press, 1990.

Bystedt, Jean, Siri Lynn and Deborah Potts. *Moderating to the Max: A Full-tilt Guide to Creative, Insightful Focus Groups and Depth Interviews.* Ithaca: Paramount Market Publishing, 2010.

Frank, Christopher and Paul Manone. *Drinking from the Fire Hose: Making Smarter Decisions Without Drowning in Information.* New York: Portfolio Hardcover, 2011.

Hair, Joseph, Mary Wolfinbarger, Robert Bush, and David Ortinau. *Essentials of Marketing Research.* New York: McGraw Hill/Irwin, 2012.

Harris, David, F. *The Complete Guide to Writing Questionnaires: How to Get Better Information for Better Decisions.* Durham: I&M Press, 2014.

Kaden, Robert, Gerald Linda, and Melvin Prince. *Leading Edge Marketing Research: 21st-Century Tools and Practices.* Los Angeles, London, New Delhi, Singapore, and Washington, D.C.: SAGE Publications, 2011.

Kahneman, Daniel. *Thinking, Fast and Slow.* New York: Farrar, Straus and Giroux, 2011.

Keegan, Sheila. *Qualitative Research: Good Decision Making through Understanding People, Cultures and Markets.* London and Philadelphia: Kogan Press, 2009.

Kotler, Philip and Kevin Keller. *Marketing Management.* Boston: Prentice Hall, 2011.

Patton, Michael Quinn. *Qualitative Research & Evaluation*

Methods. Los Angeles, London, New Delhi, Singapore, and Washington, D.C.: SAGE Publications, 2001.

Payne, Stanley. *The Art of Asking Questions.* Princeton: Princeton University Press, 2014.

Ries, Al, Jack Trout, and Philip Kotler. *Positioning: The Battle for Your Mind.* New York: McGraw-Hill, 2000.

Tourangeau, Roger, Lance Rips, and Kenneth Rasinski. *The Psychology of Survey Response.* Cambridge: Cambridge University Press, 2000.

Zaltman, Gerald. *How Customers Think: Essential Insights into the Mind of the Market.* Boston: Harvard Business School Press, 2003.

Zeisel, Hans. *Say it with Figures.* New York: HarperCollins College Div., 1985.

Zikmund, William and Barry Babin. *Essentials of Marketing Research.* Mason, OH: South-Western Cengage Learning, 2009.

APPENDIX II

Glossary

Action Grid A visualization of survey findings that enables the reader to quickly ascertain their implication for action. A common example is where two pieces of information about an item are plotted in a two-dimensional quad that shows the importance of a product attribute on the vertical axis and the degree to which survey respondents are satisfied with its performance on the horizontal axis.

B2B An abbreviation for business to business. This is where one business is selling its products and services to another business.

Banner Tables Provide a visualization of the survey data. Each question is shown on a page divided into 16 columns. The first column shows the results in percentages by the total survey sample. The remaining columns show the results by demographic subgroups (e.g., age, income, gender) or answers to other questions (e.g., those who answered "yes" to Q4). The latter provides a means of showing the possible relationship between two questions.

Big Data An all-encompassing term for any collection of data sets that are too large and complex to process using traditional data processing applications. Such data sets are collected from a diversity of sources such as scanning of purchases at retail checkouts, cameras, listening devices, software, mobile devices, etc.

Computerized Telephone Interviewing (CATI) Telephone interviewing done through a computer system. The system automatically dials phone numbers of households, both listed and unlisted, to produce a random sample of telephone households. See *Random Digit Dialing*.

Conjoint Analysis A statistical technique used in market research to determine how people value different features that characterize an individual product or service.

Consultant A person in a market research company who provides thought leadership on new business proposals and projects.

Custom Research Market research specific to a particular client and its issue, as opposed to research undertaken by the research company and sold to anyone (i.e., syndicated research).

Decision Modeling Varied analytical techniques (e.g., conjoint analysis, MaxDiff) used in survey research to model how people make choices.

Desktop Data Portal Used in market research to provide researchers and clients immediate access to survey data and reports via their desktop computers. Such systems provide graphical presentations of the data and enable users to manipulate and analyze the data, as well as create their own reports.

Dichotomous Scale Scale used in a survey question where the respondent is asked to choose one of two opposing answers (e.g., yes-no, agree-disagree, like-dislike, etc.).

Discrete Choice Modeling Often abbreviated as DCM, one of the standard analytical techniques used in decision modeling research.

Electromyography Used in neuroscience to understand how people physically react to different stimuli by measuring their facial muscles for positive and negative reactions. As used in market research, the stimuli might be exposure to advertising, products, and the like.

Enterprise Feedback Management (EFM)   Systems and software used by companies to survey customers and other constituents and link findings to their relationship management processes. Information is disseminated internally to all key stakeholders who can readily act on the information.

Focus Groups   One of a number of qualitative market research techniques. Involves a small group of individuals (typically 8-10) who meet some desired criteria based on their demographics, behavior, and/or attitudes. A trained moderator facilitates a discussion about a particular topic of interest to the sponsoring organization. May be done in-person or via the Internet.

Galvanic Skin Response (GSR)   A change in the electrical resistance of the skin occurring in moments of strong emotion; measurements of this change are commonly used in lie detector tests. Also sometimes used in market research to gauge emotional reactions to test stimuli such as advertisements, products, and the like.

In-depth Interview (IDI)   One of a number of qualitative market research techniques. Involves a one-on-one interview with individuals who meet some desired criteria based on their demographics, behavior, and/or attitudes. A trained moderator facilitates a discussion about a particular topic of interest to the sponsoring organization. May be done in-person or by phone.

Infographics   Visual representations of information, data, or knowledge intended to present complex information quickly and clearly. Increasingly used in reporting market research findings.

Interval Scale   Used in market research questions to measure the strength of feelings about something or a propensity to behave in a certain way. The interval scale typically consists of 5, 7, or 10 points, the distance between each point presumed to be equal.

Likert Scale   The most often used interval scale in surveys. The endpoints refer to polar opposite ideas. A common example is *Strongly*

Disagree (1), *Disagree* (2), *Neither Agree nor Disagree* (3), *Agree* (4), *Strongly Agree* (5).

Magnetic Resonance Imaging (MRI)   A medical technology used to measure the anatomy and physiology of the human body. Now also being used in neuroscience to map brain functions. The latter has application for new market research techniques.

Market Segmentation   Refers to the many diverse ways (e.g., demographics, attitudes, behaviors, etc.) any group of individuals may subdivide. Used in market research to identify and understand markets of interest and ways to reach them.

MaxDiff   A decision-modeling methodology used in market research to identify what people most value. Involves showing survey respondents a series of lists of product/service attributes and asking them to select the most and least liked or most and least important.

Net Promoter   A measure of customer loyalty based on asking one question—"likelihood of recommending" a product, service, brand. Used widely in surveys of customer loyalty. Developed by Fred Reichheld of Bain & Company.

Onboarding   Refers to the process through which new employees in an organization acquire the necessary knowledge, skills, and behaviors to become effective organizational members.

Panel   As used in market research, refers to groups of people who have agreed to participate in surveys, usually online. Provides a cost-effective way to sample large groups of individuals, especially when desired characteristics are of interest to the researcher.

Primary Research   New research to be conducted to study an issue, as opposed to research already done (referred to as secondary research) and available to those who have a need to access it.

Propensity Weighting   A statistical method used to make survey samples more representative of the populations they represent.

Proprietary Study　　Research commissioned by an organization for its own use only.

Pupil Dilation　　As used in market research, refers to the degree to which the pupils of those participating in a research study dilate in response to viewing some visual material such as an advertisement, product, and the like. Measures a physiological response to such stimuli believed to be indicative of one's attention or emotional reaction.

Qualitative Research　　Research that involves small samples and unstructured questioning of the research participants. The "data" are the participants' comments in response to questions posed by an interviewer.

Quantitative Research　　Research that involves large numbers of respondents and mostly structured questionnaires. The "data" are numeric and are analyzed through statistical procedures.

Random Digit Dialing (RDD)　　A technique used in telephone interviewing to randomly select households based on software that randomly generates telephone numbers. Overcomes the problem of not selecting households whose phone numbers are not listed in a published directory, should the latter be used as the sample source.

Randomization　　As applied to market research, refers to the selection of survey respondents based on chance as opposed to a systematic process.

Regression Analysis　　A statistical process for estimating the relationship among two or more variables. Used extensively in market research modeling.

Regression Techniques　　See *Regression Analysis*. Refers to the multiple ways of doing such an analysis.

Representative Sample　　A sample of survey respondents that accurately mirrors the population it is meant to represent.

Request for Proposal (RFP)   In the case of market research, a written solicitation sent by an organization to any number of other firms inviting them to prepare a proposal to conduct research. Such requests detail the background, objectives, (sometimes) the approach, desired deliverables, timing, and other relevant information needed by those who will prepare their proposals.

Response Scales   The manner in which survey respondents are asked to answer a question. Typical scales are interval (such as a 1–7 rating) or dichotomous (such as Yes/No, Like/Dislike, True/False).

Sampling Frame   Any number of sources (e.g., lists, panels, computer-generated phone numbers, etc.) used to draw a sample of people or businesses for a survey.

Screening Questions   Questions asked at the beginning of a research study to qualify people to participate, on the basis of one or more desired criteria (e.g., demographics, attitudes, behaviors, etc.).

Secondary Research   Research that already has been done and packaged, which is then accessed by individuals for study.

Strategy Grid   See *Action Grid*

Survey Instrument   Another name for a research questionnaire.

Syndicated Research   Research that is done by a research organization and then sold to anyone. The J.D. Powers Customer Satisfaction reports are well-known examples.

Testable Hypothesis   A finding in the form of an attitude or behavior from a qualitative research study that is then examined in a follow-up quantitative research study to determine how many people think and/or act that way.

Text Analysis   Software that identifies and quantifies themes in comments provided by survey responses in response to open-ended questions. The analysis also identifies the positive or negative attitude associated with each comment.

Text Analytics   See *Text Analysis.*

Thought Leadership   The role taken by individual(s) who take the lead on designing a market research study and then interpreting and reporting the results. These are usually the more senior members of the research team.

Touchpoints   The interactions that an organization has with its constituents. In business this will include things like sales, support, communications, billing, the website, etc.

Utility Maximization   An economic-psychological concept that posits that individuals seek to obtain the maximum benefit for the least expense to them in any transaction so as to optimize the resulting value to them.

Van Westendorp Price Sensitivity   A widely-used market research technique for measuring consumer price preferences. The format asks survey respondents to name the price of a product/service at which it would be too expensive, a price at which they would question its quality, a price where it is starting to become too expensive, and the price at which the product/service would be a bargain. The technique enables researchers to identify the optimal pricing.

About the Author

 Dr. Heisler's career in the market research industry spans 40 years. During this time he has held senior positions with Market Facts, ORC International, Harris Interactive, and Nielsen. Most of his career has been as a senior strategy consultant providing thought leadership on client engagements from program design through analysis, reporting, and post-research consultation to help clients act on the research. He is experienced in all aspects of B2C and B2B market research with expertise in all of the key marketing issues—market assessment, product/service design, brand strategy and customer experience. Dr. Heisler has worked with many of the leading global corporations across the CPG, financial services, technology, telecommunications, health care, industrial, professional services, and travel and leisure industries.

In addition to his strong survey research background, he is an accomplished qualitative researcher having designed and conducted hundreds of IDIs and focus group discussions with both consumers and business executives.

Dr. Heisler is currently the director of Fairleigh Dickinson University's Certificate in Market Research program to be initiated in 2015. In addition, he has given guest lectures on qualitative and quantitative market research issues at universities and speeches at market research industry conferences.

Dr. Heisler holds a Bachelor's degree in Psychology from the University of Michigan, a Master's in Psychology from DePaul University and a Doctorate in Psychology from the Illinois Institute of Technology.

Jim Heisler, PhD

Skillman, NJ

Jimheisler25@gmail.com